The Ethiopian Patriots

THE ETHIOPIAN

PATRIOTS

FORGOTTEN VOICES OF THE
ITALO–ABYSSINIAN WAR 1935–1941

by

Andrew Hilton

Foreword by W. F. Deedes

Introduction and Annotations by Richard Pankhurst

Interviews and Transcriptions by Yonatan Sahle

SPELLMOUNT

This book is dedicated to the Ethiopian Patriots

*And even though most of the great heroes have now died,
we survivors are still proud of our struggle and sacrifice
for our country's independence*

Afa-Mamher Malak Negatu,
Patriot

First published in the UK in 2007 by
Spellmount, an imprint of
The History Press
97, St George's Place,
Cheltenham, Gloucestershire GL50 3QB
www.thehistorypress.co.uk

ISBN 978 1 86227 444 0

British Library Cataloguing in Publication Data:
A catalogue record for this book is available from the British Library

Typesetting and origination by
The History Press
Printed by TJ Books, Padstow, Cornwall

MIX
Paper | Supporting
responsible forestry
FSC
www.fsc.org FSC® C013056

EU Authorised Representative: Easy Access System Europe
Mustamäe tee 50, 10621 Tallinn, Estonia
gpsr.requests@easproject.com

CONTENTS

FOREWORD

by W. F. Deedes

I remember the wonder which I felt on first arriving in Addis Ababa in September 1935. I had been sent there as a twenty-two-year-old 'Special Correspondent' by the *Morning Post* on the eve of the outbreak of war. That the Italians would invade, there was no doubt. Mussolini's political manoeuvring and recent military embarkations had set the stage for the last European attempt at empire building by the sword.

My arrival there coincided with those of journalists from far and wide, many of some distinction, notably Evelyn Waugh, then writing for the *Daily Mail*. The place was in a state of high anxiety and we were there to cover the spectacle of war. We witnessed the preparations to meet the Italian invasion, including the so-called Central Army parading before their Emperor in lion-skin capes, brandishing their weapons, and shouting their war cries – full of bravado but wholly unequal to modern warfare. We saw too, the hopelessly inadequate medical facilities that would soon be swamped with the mutilated and the dying, in a foretaste of those calamitous events that were to overtake Europe just a few years later. We took off on our own adventures, abortive expeditions to the Northern Front to cover the Abyssinian counter-attack, and strove to get our 'copy' back to our editors and the outside world.

For us it was all over by Christmas. The Italian army had conquered a large portion of the country and the story had gone cold. But for the Abyssinians it had only just begun. After we had packed up and moved on, the 'Lion of Judah' issued a desperate call to arms, before he himself was forced to take the same train that we had, down to Djibouti and into exile.

For the next five years the Abyssinian Patriots, a mixture of regular army, country militias, and peasant farmers, fought a war of resistance against the Italian occupation, largely unreported and unnoticed as larger events unfolded in Europe. With the outbreak of World War II, and spearheaded by a modern Allied force, the Patriots were able to participate in the defeat of the army of occupation and liberate their country.

Seventy years on, these personal recollections from a handful of survivors who took part in the struggle form a unique perspective on that period of resistance. They provide a fascinating insight into the day-to-day experiences of 'the ordinary man', many of them just country folk, often no more than boys (or girls), responding to the call to resist the rape of their country – many of them performing deeds of which they would never have thought themselves capable.

Ethiopia, whose people I have come to admire greatly, was extremely unfortunate to suffer the subsequent darkness of the Mengistu regime and with it the suppression of all links with its Imperial past. No room was allowed in the national memory for heroic deeds associated with the Emperor and his followers. Now that the Derg regime is itself history, this gathering together of recollections is timely as the veterans are now well into their old age, and there are fewer and fewer of them left to remember. This collection of memoirs will in part go some way towards recording, in their own words, the sacrifices that they and others like them made for future generations.

Bill Deedes

PREFACE

This book consists of the recollections of men and women who took part in the Ethiopian resistance movement during the Italo–Abyssinian War of 1935–41. There is no specific date upon which the period of resistance can be said to have started, but it is widely accepted to mean the period after the set-piece battles had been lost, when much of the country was under Italian occupation and when armed resistance was carried out by groups of militias and partisans on a sporadic and localised basis. Their long, lonely struggle is testament to their courage, determination, faith and national pride. The fighters became known simply as *Arbegnochs* or 'Patriots' and these recollections are transcripts of personal interviews with some of their surviving numbers. This is their story told in their own words.

The Death and Reburial of Haile Sellassie

This book has evolved largely by accident, through a series of chance meetings and events. The first of these occurred when I was on a business trip to Addis Ababa in November 2000. My visit coincided with the funeral of Haile Sellassie I, Emperor of Abyssinia, which I instinctively recognised as a piece of history in the making. As Bill Deedes notes in his account of the ceremony in *At War with Waugh: The Real Story of Scoop*, 'It was an unusual event in that not many men are ceremoniously buried a quarter of a century after their death.'

Following his overthrow in the revolution of 1974 by Major Mengistu Haile Miriam, the Emperor had been held prisoner in his own palace and was reported to have died the following year, aged eighty-three. The body was never released, and it was widely held that Mengistu had murdered him and dumped the corpse under the latrines, thus appealing to Mengistu's warped sense of humour as a suitably ignominious end for his arch enemy. There followed almost two decades of despotic rule, at first under the military regime of which Mengistu had emerged as leader, and then as President and Dictator of the Marxist State, which became known as the Derg regime. It was characterised by its brutality and by the deaths of tens of thousands of its citizens. After Mengistu himself was ousted in 1991, the Emperor's remains were finally recovered. It is said that a search of the palace revealed that the rumours had indeed been true and that the Emperor's remains were exhumed from a hole under a bathroom next to Mengistu's office. This is all somewhat speculative as the facts have never really come to light. Whether it was actually murder, and if so by whom, may never be known. Suffice to say that the Emperor died in mysterious circumstances and his remains were only recovered many years later.

However, the decision of what to do with the remains was a delicate one which was to take a further eight years to resolve. The Emperor's status generated a cult-like following and his continuing popularity was seen as a threat to the post-Derg government. To afford him a State Funeral would be to risk fuelling royalist sentiments, yet to refuse it would risk alienating a large section of the population. The impasse between the Memorial Foundation (which had been established representing the family, the old noble class – or what remained of them after the Mengistu regime – and royalists) and the new government was finally resolved through a compromise – a privately funded ceremony would be allowed, but not a State Funeral.

The funeral ceremony was to take place over the course of a day in three separate places of worship, starting early in the morning at the first and ending at the Holy Trinity Cathedral some time after mid-day where he would finally be laid to rest in the crypt alongside his Empress. As a result of this reluctant and limited government sanction, the ceremony had not been highly publicised and I wondered whether or not it would be worth going. Indeed, I had even been warned that I should stay away as it might turn violent if the authorities tried to interfere or somehow exert control over the crowds. However, with an eye for the historic occasion I could hardly let it pass, and the day being a Sunday with little else to occupy me I decided to take a taxi to see if I could catch a glimpse of the final stage of the procession.

Despite the lack of media publicity there was not a soul in the country who was not aware of the event and crowds lined the streets of the processional route. As the taxi drew nearer the Cathedral the crowd grew thicker and it was clear that this was not going to be the quiet affair that the government had hoped. After paying the taxi I walked towards the gates of the Cathedral grounds, becoming submerged in an ever denser crowd. I noticed that the gates were closed and controlled by police who were only allowing in those with tickets, which I then found could only be bought on the previous day. My lack of forward planning might have resulted in a very different outcome, but somehow I managed to get swept up in the swirl of people flowing through the gates and past the policemen, now swamped in their hopeless task of ticket-checking.

Inside the grounds things were a little more controlled as police with batons kept the crowd in a modicum of order, leaving open an access route to the Cathedral entrance for the funeral cortège.

I, of course, was now at the back of a seething mass of people with no chance of seeing anything. However, within minutes an old, short, wiry man dressed in traditional white robes gripped me by the elbow and cleared the way shouting 'Let him through, he's a *ferengie* [foreigner] and he's got a camera!' Before I knew it I found myself right at the front of the crowd, where my 'minder' then called upon a nearby policeman to escort me across to join the local and international press in their media 'island'. I was all set for a perfect view of the forthcoming proceedings.

Whilst I awaited the funeral cortège I was able to watch the colourful events unfold. Local dignitaries began to arrive, elders of the Orthodox Church with their fabulously embroidered robes and umbrellas, looking timeless in their attire, yet enigmatically climbing down from their four-wheel drives; foreign diplomats arriving in their CD-registered limousines; various Ethiopian VIPs; and finally Princess Tenagne Worq, the only living child of the Emperor (whom, I understand has since passed away). As they took their seats in front of the Cathedral, where the ceremony was to take place, local church groups each dressed in their own distinctive 'uniforms' added to the spectacle, waving incense sticks, singing hymns, blowing bugles and beating drums.

And then the cortège itself arrived – an eclectic collection of vehicles, the centre-piece being a flag-draped flatbed truck, bearing the coffin, itself wrapped in the distinctive green, yellow and red-striped national flag. Four members of the Emperor's personal bodyguard held post at each corner of the coffin, whilst others moved through on foot to line the final path to his burial place. Despite their advanced years, the Emperor's Bodyguard looked formidable, and exciting too in their traditional uniforms of brightly coloured flowing robes, with lion's mane headdresses, spears and leather shields – even in death guarding the body of their beloved Emperor. I was awestruck. This was not some staged event for tourists, this was a natural outpouring of love and respect, not only for their Emperor, but also for their traditional way of life. Here at the dawn of the new millennium – despite the four-wheel drives and the modern media technology – the scene was timeless; Ethiopia was staking its claim to its traditional roots. I had been expecting to merely catch a glimpse of a funeral procession, and yet here as the precious cargo was unloaded and tenderly carried to the foot of the Cathedral steps I was close enough to touch the flag-draped coffin of the Lion of Judah, surrounded by his original warriors!

Introduced to the Patriots

The coffin was placed on a dais and the ceremony was conducted by the *Abuna* (Archbishop) in front of the seated VIPs. The standing crowd strained respectfully, the better to see and hear. Some held poster-sized photographs of the Emperor, others quietly wept. Even in death, Haile Sellassie had the ability to generate passion and emotions. The ceremony was long, hours it seemed, involving speeches and traditional hymns, and then finally the coffin was hoisted once more and the procession threaded its way into the Cathedral, and presumably down to the crypt – for the rest of us were not allowed into this inner sanctum.

This had all taken much longer than I had expected. The sun was beating down mercilessly and I was now beginning to feel its effects, having come on an impulse without water, hat or sun-block. Funnily enough, in relating his experiences in *At War with Waugh*, Bill Deedes, sitting with the VIPs, describes how he too had forgotten his hat and he talks of being 'slowly roasted in the tropical sun'.

Despite the onset of mild dehydration I stayed on, as I had noticed that the crowd was not dispersing but remained, milling around in the Cathedral grounds, waiting for some further happening. People were now talking and a couple of university students approached me wanting to practise their English and to find out what I thought of the ceremony. They told me that the service would continue inside for an hour or two before a final address to the crowd outside.

Whilst we chatted and waited, I feasted my eyes on the colourful groups and individuals, the churchmen with their amazing robes and sequined umbrellas of purple and gold, ordinary folk wearing their traditional white robes and others wearing western dress, all set in a brightly sunlit tropical garden of palm trees and bougainvilleas. They took me to the small cemetery and showed me the grave of Sylvia Pankhurst, daughter of the famous English suffragette Emmeline, whom, I was later to discover, had played such an important part in supporting the Abyssinian cause in Britain. She had lobbied vocally and tirelessly from the early stages of the Italian invasion and particularly during the Emperor's period of exile, shaming the British government into action. She was to dedicate the rest of her life to Ethiopia.

I had noticed a number of elderly Ethiopian gentlemen in the crowd, dressed in a variety of old colonial-looking uniforms, some wearing pith helmets and proudly displaying rows of medals on their chests. In response to my query, my new-found friends replied, 'Oh, those are Patriots from the time of the Italian Invasion. Would you like to meet them?' And without further ado I was introduced not only to these individuals, but also their extraordinary story.

They told me of the Fascist invasion of 1935 and of how the Ethiopian regular army and a hastily raised militia had fought bravely in a series of pitched battles; of a medieval army, some on horseback, and armed only with spears, sticks and obsolete single-shot rifles pitted against the might of a twentieth-century European mechanised army, equipped with artillery, tanks and aeroplanes; of battles where 'bullets showered down like rain drops'. They told me too of how, having lost the battles, the people never gave up and, whilst the country came under foreign occupation, they became resistance fighters, or 'Patriots'. As I listened, they were amazed that a foreigner should show any interest in them and their story. After all, they told me, it was only recently that the debt they are owed has achieved some recognition. Under the Derg regime the Emperor's role in the overthrow of the Italian invasion was erased from the national memory and many of those associated with him disappeared, as did so many others, lost without trace.

But now, in a more democratic environment, the new government has at least provided some redress, such as restoring much of the land belonging to the Patriots – land that had been confiscated under the previous regime.

The Association of Ethiopian Patriots

The Patriots that I had spoken with had told me of their veterans' association and had invited me to pay them a visit at their offices and to look around their museum. Despite my heavy workload and my limited time in the country, I managed to do this. When I arrived I was received with great ceremony by the President of the Association of Ethiopian Patriots and his staff. These were not the old Patriots that I had met previously but somewhat younger military retirees who were running the Association and trying to support their older comrades as best they could. I was told that the old Patriots had little if any pension and most were dependent upon their relatives for food and shelter.

Just like the individuals whom I had met, the Association staff were delighted that a *ferengie* was interested in their own history and proudly showed me around their modest offices and their 'museum'. The latter was woefully sparse by western standards, being an empty basement room with a few old rifles, spears, and a banner or two on display – and not forgetting the stuffed horse! I asked them about their archives – administrative documents, letters, photos, memoirs, etc. They looked at me with surprise (and perhaps a little embarrassment too?). 'Well, it was not the type of warfare where we kept records, and there were no cameras, and many people could not read and write. And now that the Patriots are old they don't know how to go about writing down their memories'.

As my visit came to an end, they asked me if I would like to meet one of the more famous Patriots and so it was that I found myself meeting Captain Ayana Berre the very next day. A wonderful, charming and dignified old man of eighty, dressed in a homburg hat and grey, somewhat frayed, suit. His firm handshake was that of a younger man and belied the need for his walking stick. We poured over maps and talked (through an interpreter) of places where he had seen action. He traced the route that he had taken in 1941 with the Emperor's army as it made its way from the Sudan to relieve Addis Ababa, liberating the land from its oppressors along the way. He had been attached to the British 'Gideon Force' under Orde Wingate as a liaison officer and knew the famous Major (subsequently Major-General) well. He was very precise about details and became animated and excited by his recollections. It was a meeting that was enjoyed by all. 'Official' photographs were taken, and hands were heartily shaken all round, but it was clear to me that it could not end here. There was an urgent need to record Captain Ayana Berre's memories, and not just his, but those of his compatriots too. I resolved there and then to somehow create an oral record for the museum, and for posterity.

The Team

For this task I would need some local input and my first move was to look up the telephone number of Richard Pankhurst, son of Sylvia, and Professor at the Institute of Ethiopian Studies in Addis Ababa, who is generally regarded as the local authority on all things Ethiopian. He listened whilst I briefly explained my idea over the phone and finally said, 'Yes, well you must come around for tea so that we can talk about it.'

Addis is not much on street names, but with my driver to ask the way we eventually found his home. I spent a delightful afternoon discussing what had now become our mutual passion whilst Rita, Richard's charming wife, served tea and biscuits in the shade of their gazebo in their green and sunny tropical African garden. It was Richard's enthusiasm that really got the idea going, and we agreed that the only practical way to undertake the project would be to recruit a local person, someone who would be capable of carrying out the interviews in at least one, and probably more, of the local languages. Richard agreed to help however he could, and would see about finding a suitable student.

On the way back to the office, my driver, impressed with seeing such an important national figure, asked me what was going on. I told him about our discussion 'Well!' he exclaimed 'My son is a history undergraduate, and is fluent in English as well as the local languages. He would love to assist with the interviews.' What a coincidence! This was too good to be true! A brief meeting the next day and I was satisfied that Yonatan Sahle was just the person for the job. The team was complete.

The Interviews

With the help of the Association we arranged to meet the first of the interviewees. As I sat in on that first interview, unable to understand a word, but able to see how Yonatan bonded with the old veteran, I knew that we were lucky to have him on board. It was a pleasure to see the distance between the generations evaporate as details of some ancient battle were discussed and ironed out – 'No, no, it was like this ...' the Patriot was saying, arms flailing as he illustrated his point.

I returned to the UK safe in the knowledge that the project was in good hands. Yonatan was able to trace and personally interview fourteen veterans in Addis Ababa between 2003 and 2004. Notes were taken during the interviews and all were tape-recorded, transcribed and then translated. I have made editorial corrections, but I have tried to keep the manuscripts intact, despite some slightly curious English, as this captures the essence of how the Ethiopians speak – it is, after all, 'in their own words'.

At the time of the interviews the veterans were then mostly in their early eighties, the youngest being seventy-seven and the oldest being ninety-one years of age. Many would have only been in their mid-teens when they joined the resistance. They often spoke of their fathers, uncles and brothers with whom they fought, giving us a unique insight into the family nature of the patriotic movement, and of strong allegiances to local leaders. The interviews provided other common threads: the hardships of living in the bush, the sense of military isolation, the support of the local population and their fierce sense of patriotism. These Patriots look back now with humour at their ragged dress and bare feet, but there is no humour when recollecting wounds suffered from artillery shells and aerial bombardments with mustard gas, when the chances of surviving if wounded – having no medical supplies or hygienic shelter – were minimal. Passions still run high, and for them, despite the passage of time, this is not history but a living thing. The Italian invasion and occupation was to them as vile as the Nazi invasion of Europe was to the European nations – and in many ways, along with the Spanish Civil War, it may be viewed as the opening chapter of the Second World War. The British-led counter-invasion five years later had the same resonance for them as the D-Day landings had for us in the West.

One interesting aspect which came to light during the interviews was the popularity of 'chanting songs'. It seems that after some incident or contact with the enemy, the Patriots would make up songs relating the events and characters involved. I have included some that were sung for us, though the meaning may sometimes be a little obscure now. Nicknames too were common, especially for leaders, who are often referred to by their 'horse name' – the Ethiopian equivalent of a 'nom de guerre'.

The Patriots were asked if they had any particular memories of exciting actions or battles they were involved in, with some curious results. Often, rather than being embarrassed or self-effacing, they would reply 'Oh yes! One heroic deed that I remember doing ...' Such boasting seems somewhat indiscreet to the European ear, where the word 'heroic' is normally reserved for use when describing the deeds of others. It also belies the general demeanour and composure of the narrators who were not 'boasting' in the way that we would normally associate with the word. I was curious as to why this was so. I discovered the answer whilst trawling through the photographic archive at the Imperial War Museum where I came across pictures of 'Boasting Ceremonies'.

This was the practice of individuals retelling and reliving their heroism in battle, whilst others stood or sat around and listened, each taking his turn in the circle. In this way their deeds must have entered into the local folklore, something akin to the Viking and Greek sagas. However, for the sake of the flow of the manuscript the word 'heroic' has been amended in most cases.

The Patriots were also keen to talk about the need for the current youth of Ethiopia to be active in defending its borders, and many Patriots rounded off their interviews with comments or advice on this. Such remarks might at first seem odd, until one realises that at the time of the interviews Ethiopia was involved in a serious border dispute with neighbouring Eritrea. This dispute is viewed in Ethiopia as yet another act of aggression against its sovereignty. As *Woizero* Alemitu Mekonnen puts it in Chapter 5, 'Let God protect my country, Ethiopia, and make its borders fire, and its interior paradise'. The veterans were aware too of their ever dwindling numbers and thanked God, genuinely, in accordance with their Orthodox upbringing, for being blessed with a long life.

Once the translations were completed I spoke with Richard about binding the transcripts in order to present them to the Association. Ever the true academic, he exclaimed 'Nonsense! We must publish!' And so began the task of turning the transcripts into a book. We quickly agreed upon the need to have a Foreword written by someone with a well-known involvement with the country during that period. Who better than Bill Deedes! In 1935 the intrepid young reporter had waited in Addis Ababa for the invasion to begin, and had covered the story from the inside. He had been there too, at the funeral ceremony, covering the story for *The Daily Telegraph*. To compliment this Foreword, Richard Pankhurst has written the Introduction which provides a concise yet valuable summary of the historical context from which to better appreciate these recollections.

From Generation to Generation

And that is how this book came into being. It is not intended to be a history of the Italo–Abyssinian war – there are other excellent in-depth academic accounts of this. It is a collection of personal recollections made by men and women nearly seventy years after the events they are relating. Each has a story to tell and each tells it in his or her own words. Only Captain Ayana Berre was a career soldier, though many went on to have military careers after the war.

The story of the Patriots is mainly that of peasant farmers, women, boys and girls living in the countryside but willing to take up arms against a foreign invader, as their forefathers had done countless times before them. This is what makes their stories so interesting and meaningful.

I found that occasionally their stories contain factual errors or inconsistencies with regard to dates, personalities and, in particular, activities on the political stage. These may result from the fact that the Patriots were operating as irregular units often in isolation, living off the land, where no diaries were kept and communications with the outside world and knowledge of the 'big picture' were at best sporadic. Like so many foot-soldiers, they survived on a diet of rumour and speculation, more interested in their next meal, survival, and tactical successes than the overall strategy. Some of the errors in their narratives may be a result of failing memories – one of the problems of relying on recollections after the passage of such a long time. This has been exacerbated where memories have not been kept alive by the constant retelling of stories. In so many societies now, the younger generation is not interested in the stories of 'the old folk' – until it is too late. I have heard so many times, in other parts of Africa, the laments for past times when families used to sit around the fire and the elders held a special place in their families and communities as they passed on their tribal, family and personal histories. The attractions of television, radio, and the city lights have all contributed to a decline in the interaction between the generations and to the loss of unrecorded stories. In Ethiopia, the problem was made worse by the Derg regime actively discouraging anything which would perpetuate the mythology surrounding the Emperor.

This collection is therefore the result of an urgent initial response to record something, however incomplete, of the Patriots' memories before such stories are lost forever – In the short period since the interviews were recorded, I am sad to say that Sergeant Hunegnaw Herera has passed away. One can't help but feel that much more could be done. The interviews took place in only one sitting each and there is scope for recording greater numbers and allowing for greater depth. There is also an urgent need to provide support to those veterans in need and to the Association and its museum. This is something that we are working on in our small way and we may look to establish a website to assist with this.

However, if our purpose has been to capture something of the past for future generations, then the most dramatic evidence of this was actually demonstrated during the interviews themselves. What a pleasure it was to see the interaction of Yonatan, our young Ethiopian historian, enthusiastically bonding with people more than sixty years his senior. They in turn shed their years – and sometimes tears – as memories flooded back and they relived the times when they were young and full of passion for their cause: the defence of their country against a foreign invader.

A.H.
Hvar, Croatia

ACKNOWLEDGEMENTS

In undertaking this project I have received encouragement from a great many people, too numerous to thank individually, but my heartfelt thanks to you nonetheless. In particular I would like to thank the following:

The President and members of the Association of Ethiopian Patriots, especially *Ato* Teklemika'el Kidanemariam (who has sadly passed away), *Ato* Workneh Tegegn, and *Ato* Addamu Asegahegn, for their warm hospitality, for facilitating the interviews and for the splendid work they are doing; Bill Deedes for agreeing to provide a Foreword at what was a difficult time for him during his illness. It is a great loss that he passed away this summer and he will be missed by more people than we would dare to guess at. It is an honour to include within these pages what may be his last 'despatch'.

Thank you to Yvonne Oliver at the Imperial War Museum Photographic Archive for granting permission to reproduce photos; David Rowley at Corbis; Anthony Mockler for his permission to reproduce the map showing the route of the Emperor's return and extracts of the Chronology from his excellent book *Haile Selassie's War*; Nick Rankin; Susan Corning; John Leigh; and all at Spellmount Publishers for their help and guidance.

I would also like to acknowledge the highly valuable contributions from Richard Pankhurst, for assistance with the editing and the numerous inputs on Ethiopian matters, for writing the Introduction which provides such a useful historical background from which to appreciate these recollections, for his unfailing enthusiasm, and for his insistence that the material be published; and of course Yonatan Sahle for all his efforts and good work in carrying out the interviews, transcriptions and translations with such enthusiasm and dedication.

Finally, I would like to thank the Patriots for sharing their memories with us and with whom it has been such a pleasure and a privilege to meet, and without whom this book would not have been possible – this book is dedicated to them.

Information about the Authors/Contributors

Andrew Hilton is a Consultant Chartered Surveyor who travels extensively, especially within Africa, in connection with his work with international economic development programmes. He is a graduate of Birkbeck College, London, in Field Archaeology, and has a keen interest in military and oral history.

Richard Pankhurst is a scholar and educator who has lived in Ethiopia for more than thirty years. He is the Founder and first Director of the Institute of Ethiopian Studies of Addis Ababa University, formerly Haile Sellassie I University, and Founder-Chair of its Society of Friends. Professor Pankhurst is a prolific and respected author of numerous publications dealing with the history of Ethiopia.

Yonatan Sahle is a graduate of Alemaya University, where he earned a distinction in History. He currently teaches at Arba Minch University in southern Ethiopia and is undertaking graduate studies in Archaeology at the College of Social Sciences, Addis Ababa University.

GLOSSARY

Abbo   A church

Abujedid   Loosely woven imported cloth

Addis Ababa   Literally 'New Flower', the Ethiopian
                     capital city

Amhara   The ruling ethnic group. Their language
                     is Amharic

Arbegnoch   Patriot

Awraja   Administrative district, or sub-province,
                     within a province

Banda   The Italian term for a group or band
                     of soldiers, and by extension in the
                     Ethiopian context, irregular or 'native'
                     troops in Italian service

Birr   Unit of currency, literally in Amharic
                     'silver'

Demera	A pile of poles and branches used for a bonfire at the Meskel feast
Ensat	A false banana, a fruit similar to a banana
Fanno	A band of soldiers or Patriots
Ferengie	A European, or foreigner
Fido	Short trousers, worn by many of the Patriots
Gabi	Thickish, locally produced blanket woven from cotton thread and worn as a toga
Galla	A large ethnic group, now more often called Oromo. Their language is Gallinya, or Oromifa
Gasha	Shield made of leather; also an area of land equivalent to approximately 40 hectares
Gebbar	Tenant farmer of low status
Goddere	Root crop similar to potato
Haile Sellassie	Name of the Emperor, literally 'Power of the Trinity'
Hamasen	A district or ethnic group in highland Eritrea, and by extension, units from there fighting with the Italians

Horse name	A name adopted by warriors and nobles, similar to the French '*Nom de Guerre*'
Ircot	Leather thong, used when carrying supplies or heavy loads
Jambo	The Swahili word of greeting, equivalent to 'Hello'. Ethiopians, hearing it uttered by British troops coming from Kenya, used it by extension to mean the British.
Kebele	Local administrative district within a *woreda*
Kili	Recycled bullet
Meskel	Religious celebration commemorating the finding of the True Cross by the Byzantine Empress Helena
Naft	Rifle (see note on Firearms below)
Naftegna	A local elite, so called due to their possession of *nafts*, or rifles
Negaret	War drum
Tekel	The name of the Emperor's horse, for which reason the Emperor was known by the horse name 'Abba Tekel' or the shortened version 'Tekel'

Teff	Grain used in making the local pancake-like bread
Tej	Locally produced mead
Tella	Locally produced beer
Woreda	Administrative sub-district of an *awraja*
Ye'arada Zebegna	City security unit, called after the Arada district of Addis Ababa
Yewist Arbegnoch	Literally 'Inside Patriots', civilian supporters or spies

Note on Titles

Ethiopian Military Titles
(in order of their importance):

Negus Negusti/Atse	King of Kings/Monarch
Negus	King
Le'ul Ras	Prince, literally 'Princely Ras'
Ras	The highest title next to the *Negus*/Head of Army /Commander-in-Chief. Normally obtained through merit, not lineage

Dejazmach/Dejach	An honorific title, often given to a Provincial Governor, or Commander of the Main Body (of a force)
Fitawrari	Literally 'Commander of the Advance Guard' (of a force)
Kegnazmach/Kenyazmach	Literally 'Commander of the Right Wing' (of a force)
Grazmach/Geraz	Literally 'Commander of the Left Wing' (of a force)
Shalaka	Commander of 1,000 men (corresponding to Major)
Azazh	**Commander**
Shambal	Lesser title (corresponding to Captain)
Balambaras	Literally, 'Commander of an *amba*', (i.e. a mountain), often serving as a natural fortress

Other Titles (non-military):

Abba	Literally 'Father', title used for a priest or bishop
Abuna	Archbishop
Afa-Mamher	Learned priest

Agafari	Government supervisor
Ato	Mister
Balabat	Local chief appointed to administrative office by the government
Bitwaded	Imperial counsellor and most favoured courtier
Ichege	Traditionally the Patriarch or Head of the Ethiopian Orthodox Church
Lij	Literally 'child', a courtesy title given to a young nobleman, or prince
Mekwanent/Makonnen	Nobleman, normally a rank obtained through merit or service
Shum	Appointed local chief, or, occasionally, lord
Woizero	Lady or Noblewoman; a diminishing title, traditionally a Princess but now may mean any married woman

Note on Firearms

The Ethiopian Patriots, like many Ethiopians in the late nineteenth and early twentieth century, were familiar with a number of different types of rifle for which they coined or adapted distinctive names.

The first breech-loading rifle to reach Ethiopia, in the second half of the nineteenth century, was the British Snider. It made such an impression that the term Snider came to be virtually synonymous with breech-loader. American Remingtons, which gained considerable currency later in the century, were thus referred to as **Sniders**, or **Senadirs**.

The Italian **Wetterli**, which was sometimes so called, was also highly regarded for its rapid rate of fire. It was on that account likened to a **Wechefo**, or hurricane, and thus given that name. A Wechefo with a ring, or *maser*, of *nas* (brass) was distinguished from other such guns by being called **Nas Maser**.

Several other rifles came to be known by their place of origin. For example Russian guns, such as the Kropatschek or Berdan, were spoken of as **Moskob**, the Amharic designation for Russia. Guns from Belgium were known as **Belgig** (from the French, 'Belgique'), while those used by the Italian Alpini, or Alpine troops, were referred to as **Albin**.

Other weapons again were known by their original names, which were, however, significantly distorted. The most popular French rifle, the Fusil Gras, thus became the **Wujigra**. The Austrian Manlicher was called the **Minishir**; and the British Lee-Metford, the **Demetfer**. The Mauser, which was widely used by Ethiopian troops at the time of the invasion, was known as the **Mauzer**, and the Lebel, the **Leben**.

See Richard Pankhurst, 'Linguistic and Cultural Data on the Penetration of Fire-arms in Ethiopia', *Journal of Ethiopian Studies* (1971), IX, 1, pp. 47-82.

Note on Spelling and Country Nomenclature

Amharic names do not transcribe precisely and this has led to a wide divergence in English transcriptions, particularly of Ethiopian place names, and also the inconsistent use of double characters. Hence a number of different spellings may be encountered, for example *Kegnazmach/Kenyazmach*, *Bure/Burye*, *Sellassie/Selasie*, *Mai Chaw/Mai Cew/Maychew*, etc. The spellings adopted in the text are ones in common occurrence, or ones of personal preference, and so these may differ from spellings found in other sources.

Also, regarding Amharic names, individuals only have one name as there are no family names as such. Each individual's name is followed by his or her father's name, thus Tafari Makonnen is Tafari the son of Makonnen.

Many foreigners know – or knew – the country as Abyssinia, however, the inhabitants themselves have always called it Ethiopia. The two names have therefore been interspersed within the text.

Note on Photographs of the Interviewees

The photographs at the beginning of each chapter are from the author's private collection, with the exception of chapter 1 which was supplied by *Dejazmch* Takla-Maryam Abayere, and chapter 6 which was supplied by Patrick De Roo (www.patrickderoo.be).

INTRODUCTION

by Richard Pankhurst

The story of the Ethiopian Patriots, who fought almost alone against the Italian Fascist occupation of their country in the late 1930s, has never been adequately told and is today largely forgotten. However, the struggle of the Patriots, who kept the flag of Ethiopian independence flying throughout the enemy occupation, deserves an honoured chapter in the history of their country. The Patriots, moreover, were of major importance in the overall history of World War II; for it was their existence which enabled the Allies to rapidly defeat the common enemy in east Africa. Allied troops thus achieved their first victory of the war and succeeded in keeping Britain's sea route to the East open at a time when Italo–German strategy was to crush north-east Africa in a pincer movement based on Italian Libya to the north and Italian-occupied Ethiopia to the south.

How – and when – did the drama start?

Ethiopia, an age-old state located in east Africa, between the Red Sea and the Great African Rift Valley, had almost alone survived the European 'Scramble for Africa'. The country, by the early Twentieth Century, was the only indigenous independent state on the African continent. Italy, which had overrun part of Ethiopia in the late 1880s, had, however, established two adjacent colonies: Eritrea to the north and Italian Somalia to the south. The Italians had in fact attempted to seize the whole of the country but had been defeated by the Ethiopian Emperor Menelik at the battle of Adwa in 1896.

Italo–Ethiopian relations after Adwa had initially been peaceful, but some Italians hankered for a war of revenge, and the Italian Fascist dictator Benito Mussolini's seizure of power in 1922 soon opened a new era of conflict. Ten years later in 1932 the Duce – as he liked to be called – decided to attack Ethiopia. He declared to the world his intention to avenge Adwa and to win for Italy a 'Place in the [African] Sun'.

Mussolini's fully mechanised armies, which had overwhelming superiority in fire-power, as well as total control of the air, launched their invasion – without any declaration of war – on 3 October 1935. They attacked from both Italian colonies: Eritrea in the north and Italian Somalia in the south. The League of Nations, in Geneva, found Italy guilty of aggression, and imposed sanctions against her. These, however, proved ineffective, and failed to stop the invasion.

The Italians, violating an international agreement signed in 1926, made extensive use of poison gas, which proved decisive and broke Ethiopian resistance. The Ethiopian ruler, Emperor Haile Sellassie, who had made his way north to resist the main Italian attack from Italian Eritrea, was defeated at the battle of Mai Chaw, on 31 March 1936. Withdrawing to the Ethiopian capital, Addis Ababa, he left a fortnight later on 2 May for exile in Britain. Travelling to Geneva, he made a moving appeal to the League of Nations on 30 June. The international community, however, chose to ignore this appeal and soon abandoned sanctions against the invader, but the United States, the Soviet Union and Mexico refused to recognise the Italian 'conquest'. Though rejected at Geneva, the Emperor remained in close, if sporadic, contact with his compatriots, both in their own country and in exile, notably in the Sudan and other neighbouring territories. Unable to share in the fighting, as many Patriots would have wished, he remained a symbol of Ethiopian resistance, and a rallying point for when the day of liberation eventually dawned.

Ethiopian resistance to the Invader – later the Occupying Power – falls into three distinct, but overlapping, phases. Some Ethiopians fought, as we shall see, throughout the entire period, from 3 October 1935, when the Italian invasion began, to 27 November 1941, when the Italians finally surrendered at Gondar, while others, for one reason or another, fought in only one or two phases.

The first of these three phases of resistance ran for around seven months, from the opening of hostilities early in October 1935 to the Italian occupation of Addis Ababa on 5 May 1936. Resistance during this period was mainly conceived and organised by the Emperor, and conducted on two fronts by his pre-war army. This began to disintegrate after the battle of Mai Chaw at the end of March 1936, when many soldiers returned heartbroken to their homes.

The second phase of resistance, with which the ensuing reminiscences are mainly concerned, covers the considerably longer four-year period from the fall of Addis Ababa early in May 1936 to 10 June 1940 – the date when the Duce, seeking a seat at a future Peace Conference after the Italo–German victory he expected, most rashly entered the European war by declaring war on Britain and France. This period witnessed the emergence of a new force of Ethiopian Freedom Fighters, who fought alone without any external help. Although poorly armed, they were indomitable in spirit, and even attempted (unsuccessfully) to recapture Addis Ababa during the rainy season of July–August 1936. They increased greatly in numbers after 19 February 1937, when an attempt on the life on the Italian Viceroy, Rodolfo Graziani, by two Ethiopians of Eritrean origin, Abraha Deboch and Moges Asgedom, was followed by the three-day Addis Ababa massacre in which Italians killed thousands of innocent men, women and children. Many of the survivors thereupon fled the capital to join the resistance. The Patriots, to the distress of the Duce (as revealed to the latter's son-in-law Count Ciano) were then operating in most parts of the country, most notably in Shawa, Lasta, Gojjam, Tegray, Charchar and Yergalam. They had the secret support of Internal Patriots in Addis Ababa and other towns, who helped them obtain weapons and medical supplies. Most of the Ethiopian countryside was in fact controlled by the Patriots and their supporters, the Italians being confined to the towns and the principal roads where they could travel, and even there only under armed convoy.

The third, and shortest, phase of resistance ran from Mussolini's disastrous entry into the European war early in June 1940, through the Allied capture of Addis Ababa on 6 April 1941, and the Emperor's return to the capital on 5 May, to the final Italian surrender towards the end of November. This last phase of the war was characterised above all by British, and to a lesser extent some other Allied, involvement in the struggle. The Patriots, whose ceaseless and apparently unconquerable resistance had largely demoralised the enemy, now at last had allies – and military support – from outside their country. They no longer had to rely as they had in the past upon weapons captured from the enemy.

Emperor Haile Sellassie, who had spent most of his exile in Bath, England, was meanwhile flown by the British to the Sudan to lead the Ethiopian Liberation Campaign, mainly into Gojjam. There he had the loyal support of two British officers, Colonel Daniel Sandford and Major Orde Wingate. The latter duly served as the Emperor's Field Commander. The British Royal Air Force also collaborated by dropping leaflets despatched in Haile Sellassie's name to the Patriots and Ethiopian people in general.

The Emperor's campaign, and that of the by now victorious Patriots, was part of a three-pronged Allied attack initiated in the second half of January 1941, which brought about the collapse of the much-vaunted Fascist East African empire in only a matter of months.

The first attack began on 19 January, when British and Indian troops under General William Platt crossed the Sudanese frontier at Kassala and advanced into Eritrea. Winning the fiercely fought battle of Keren, they proceeded to capture Asmara, and then advanced victoriously into the northern Ethiopian province of Tegray.

The second attack, which opened on the following day, 20 January, was that of the Emperor, who had the support of a small army composed of Ethiopian refugees, British regulars and units from the Sudanese Defence Force. Crossing the frontier from the Sudan near the Ethiopian village of Um Idla (where Haile Sellassie raised the Ethiopian flag) they were soon joined by increasing numbers of Ethiopian Patriots. They then advanced to Debra Markos, in Gojjam, before proceeding almost to the outskirts of Addis Ababa. They later served significantly in 'mopping-up' operations, in Dessie, Jimma, Gore, Debra Tabor, Amba Alarge, and Gondar – indeed, throughout much of the country.

The third attack started only four days later, on 24 January 1941, when British and South African soldiers under General Alan Cunningham crossed from Kenya into Italian Somalia, and advanced to capture first Mogadishu and then Harar, enabling them finally to win the race to recapture Addis Ababa – which they did on 6 April.

The contribution of the Patriots to the overall campaign, though insufficiently recognised at the time, was undoubtedly considerable. During their long, lone struggle they had done much to demoralise and immobilise the enemy, who, isolated from far-off Italy, and beleaguered by the Patriots in fortified posts, were in many instances in no position to resist the Allied onslaught. Besides dominating their own central front in Gojjam, the Patriots had a major influence in 'softening up' the Italians on the northern and southern fronts before contributing greatly to the final 'mopping-up' in the country at large.

But, now, let the Patriots speak for themselves and tell us what they remember over sixty years on!

CHRONOLOGY

3 April 1930	*Negus* Tafari proclaimed *Negus Negusti* (King of Kings) and Lion of Judah under the throne name of Haile Sellassie.
2 November 1930	Coronation of the new Emperor and Empress in Addis Ababa before a large number of international delegates.
5 December 1934	The 'Incident' at Wal Wal in the Ogaden Desert – 107 Ethiopians killed during the incursion from Italian Somaliland.
9 December 1934	Ethiopia appeals by telegram to the League of Nations.
3 October 1935	An Italian army 100,000 strong commanded by General de Bono crosses the Eritrean frontier.

7 October 1935	Adwa is occupied by the Italians without fighting.
17 October 1935	The Army of the Centre, commanded by *Ras* Mulugueta sets out from Addis Ababa for the north.
8 November 1945	Makalle, the capital of the 'traitor' Haile Selassie Gugsa, is occupied by the Italians without fighting.
18 November 1935	The Emperor moves his headquarters and the Guard north to Dessie, the capital of Wallo.
19 November 1935	The League of Nations imposes sanctions on Italy.
26 November 1935	De Bono, created Marshal, is sent home in disgrace for advancing too slowly and is replaced by General Badoglio.
15 December 1935 – 23 January 1936	The First Battle of Tembien. The armies of *Ras* Kassa and *Ras* Seyoum attempt to break through the Italian defences.
6–23 January 1936	On the Southern Front General Graziani defeats *Ras* Desta and drives back his forces.
10–15 February 1936	Badoglio launches four divisions in a successful attack on *Ras* Mulugueta.

27–30 February 1936	The Second Battle of Tembien. The Italians scale the mountain peaks and drive back *Ras* Kassa and *Ras* Seyoum.
2 March 1936	*Ras* Imru, on the Ethiopian left in the Shire district, nearly defeats the advancing Italians but is in the end routed by mustard gas and incendiary bombs.
21 March 1936	The Emperor, now joined by *Ras* Kassa and *Ras* Seyoum, sets up his headquarters in a cave overlooking the plain of Lake Ashangi.
31 March 1936	The Battle of Maychew (Mai Ceu). The Emperor and armies attack six divisions commanded by Badoglio in person in the traditional Ethiopian mass frontal assault.
1 April 1936	In the West, Gondar, the historic capital of the Empire, falls to General Starace without a battle.
2 April 1936	The Emperor at last orders a retreat which, under bombardment from Italian planes and attack by horsemen of the collaborator Raya Galla, becomes a rout.
14–30 April 1936	Graziani advances in the Ogaden.

2 May 1936	Returning to Addis Ababa, the Emperor leaves by train for Djibuti.
5 May 1936	Badoglio's column enters Addis Ababa.
8 May 1936	Graziani's forces occupy Harar.
9 May 1936	Mussolini announces the conquest and annexation of Ethiopia – and proclaims King Vittorio Emanuele III the new King-Emperor.
21 May 1936	Graziani reaches Addis Ababa. Badoglio resigns voluntarily and Graziani is appointed by the Duce to rule the conquered country.
1 June 1936	Italy's possessions in the Horn of Africa are reorganised into five provinces of Africa Orientale Italiana, with Graziani – promoted to Marshal – as Viceroy.
3 June 1936	Haile Sellassie arrives in Britain.
30 June 1936	Haile Sellassie addresses the Assembly of the League of Nations in Geneva, appealing in vain for aid.
15 July 1936	Sanctions against Italy officially abandoned by the League of Nations.

19 February 1937	The final battle of the war, at Gogetti. *Dejaz* Beiene Merid and *Dejaz* Gabre Mariam defeated and shot.
19 February 1937	Assassination attempt on the Viceroy, Marshal Graziani. Followed by three days of massacres by Blackshirts in the capital, and by numerous executions of Ethiopians all over the country.
20 May 1937	297 monks of Debre Libanos, Ethiopia's most famous monastery, shot on Graziani's orders – an atrocity that leads gradually to uprisings throughout the Empire.
November 1937	As revolts spread through Gojjam and Begemder after the rains, the Duke of Aosta is appointed Viceroy to replace Graziani.
March–April 1938	Increased military activity by the Italians includes a 60,000-man 'invasion' of Gojjam in an attempt to stamp out resistance.
12 May 1938	Haile Sellassie addresses the League of Nations for a second time.
8 March 1939	Duke of Aosta is reprimanded by Mussolini for failing to fully subdue the country.

3 September 1939 Britain and France declare war on Germany. Italy remains neutral.

5 March 1940 Abebe Aregai and 20,000 Patriots attempt to ambush Vice Governor General, General Nasi, at 'peace talks' in the hills.

10 June 1940 Mussolini declares war on a defeated France and defiant but weakened Britain.

14 June 1940 The first shot of the 'Ethiopian Campaign' fired from Gallabat Fort, Sudan, by Bimbashi Hanks. After ten minutes' surprised and shocked silence, the Italians across the border at Metemma return fire.

2 July 1940 Haile Sellassie arrives in Khartoum.

August–September 1940 The Italians invade the Sudan, Kenya, and British Somaliland.

6 November 1940 Major Orde Wingate, chosen by Anthony Eden (Britain's War Minister) and General Wavell as a catalyst for the revolt inside Ethiopia, arrives in Khartoum with a million pounds and orders to work in close liaison with Haile Sellassie.

19 January 1941 British forces under General Platt recapture Kassala without a battle.

20 January 1941	The Emperor, *Ras* Kassa and Wingate's Gideon Force cross the frontier at Um Idla (Omedla) and raise the Ethiopian flag on Ethiopian soil.
2 February 1941	The Battle of Keren begins in Eritrea. Fierce fighting over impregnable mountain peaks; repeated assaults by two British Indian Infantry Divisions driven back.
11 February 1941	General Cunningham's forces from Kenya invade Italian Somaliland.
4 March 1941	Gideon Force drives Colonel Natale out of Burye.
16 March 1941	The Royal Navy recaptures British Somaliland.
27 March 1941	The Battle of Keren ends, with the Italians pulling out during the night.
29 March 1941	Cunningham's forces enter Harar.
3 April 1941	Gideon Force drives Colonel Maraventano out of Debra Markos, the capital of Gojjam.
5 April 1941	Cunningham's troops occupy Addis Ababa.
6 April 1941	The Emperor enters Debra Markos.

26 April 1941	Dessie, the capital of Wollo, falls to Brigadier Pienaar's South Africans.
1 May 1941	The Emperor stops to pray at the famous monastery of Debre Libanos, near Fiche.
5 May 1941	The Emperor returns to Addis Ababa, five years to the day after the Italians occupied it.
19 May 1941	The Duke of Aosta and 5,000 Italian troops surrender at Amba Alagi.
27 November 1941	General Nasi finally surrenders after holding out at Gondar.

(Source: Anthony Mockler, *Haile Selassie's War*)

MAPS

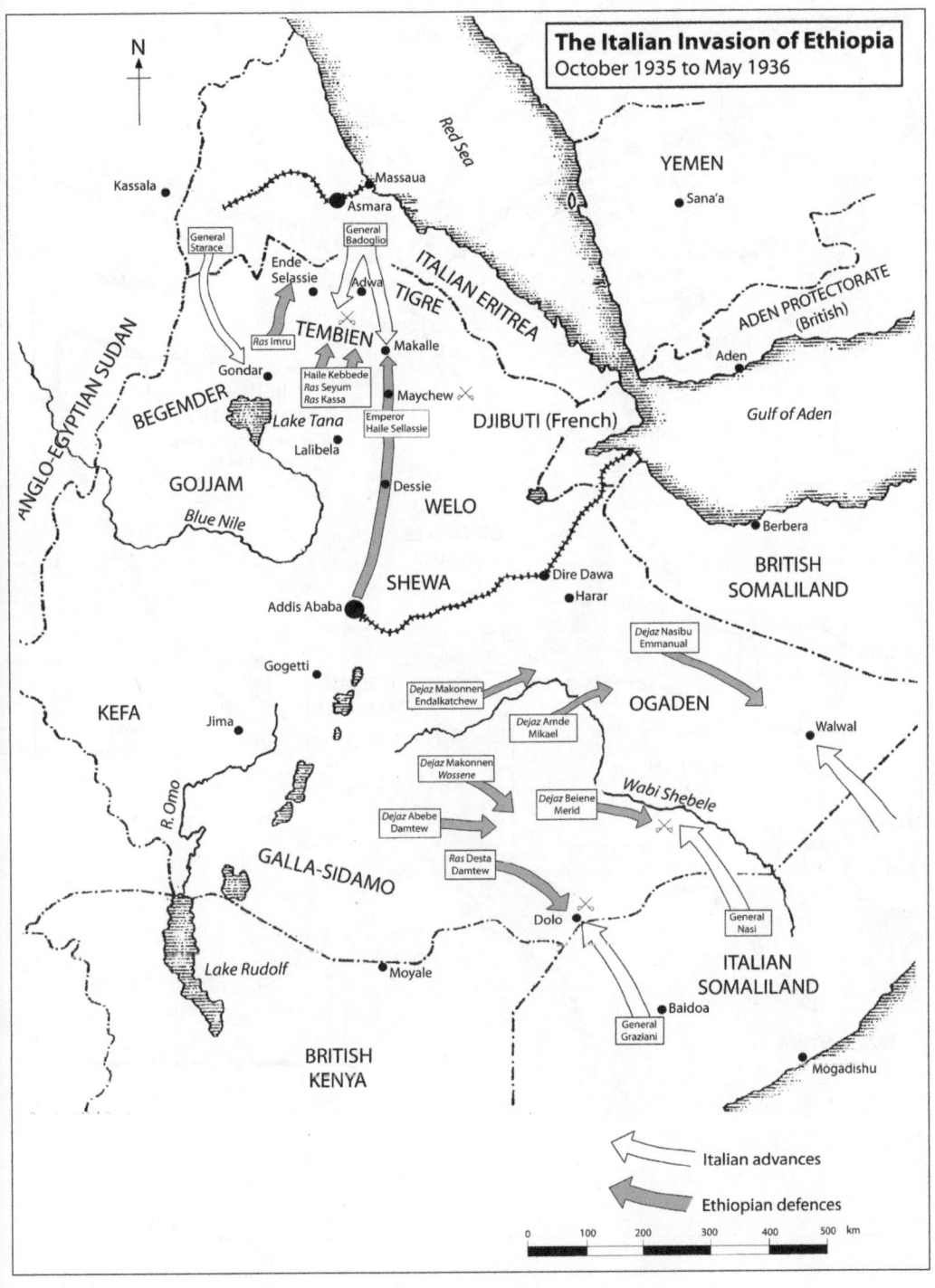

The Italian Invasion of Ethiopia
October 1935 to May 1936

N

Kassala

Red Sea

YEMEN

Sana'a

Massaua

Asmara

General
Starace

General
Badoglio

Ende
Selassie

Adwa

ITALIAN ERITREA

TIGRE

ADEN PROTECTORATE
(British)

Ras Imru

TEMBIEN

Makalle

Aden

Gondar

Haile Kebbede
Ras Seyum
Ras Kassa

Maychew

DJIBUTI (French)

Gulf of Aden

BEGEMDER

Lake Tana

ANGLO-EGYPTIAN SUDAN

Emperor
Haile Sellassie

Lalibela

GOJJAM

Dessie

WELO

Blue Nile

Berbera

SHEWA

Dire Dawa

BRITISH
SOMALILAND

Addis Ababa

Harar

Dejaz Nasibu
Emmanual

Gogetti

Dejaz Makonnen
Endalkatchew

OGADEN

KEFA

Jima

Dejaz Amde
Mikael

Walwal

Dejaz Makonnen
Wossene

R. Omo

Dejaz Abebe
Damtew

Wabi Shebele

Dejaz Beiene
Merid

GALLA-SIDAMO

Ras Desta
Damtew

General
Nasi

ITALIAN
SOMALILAND

Dolo

Lake Rudolf

Moyale

BRITISH
KENYA

General
Graziani

Baidoa

Mogadishu

Italian advances

Ethiopian defences

0   100   200   300   400   500 km

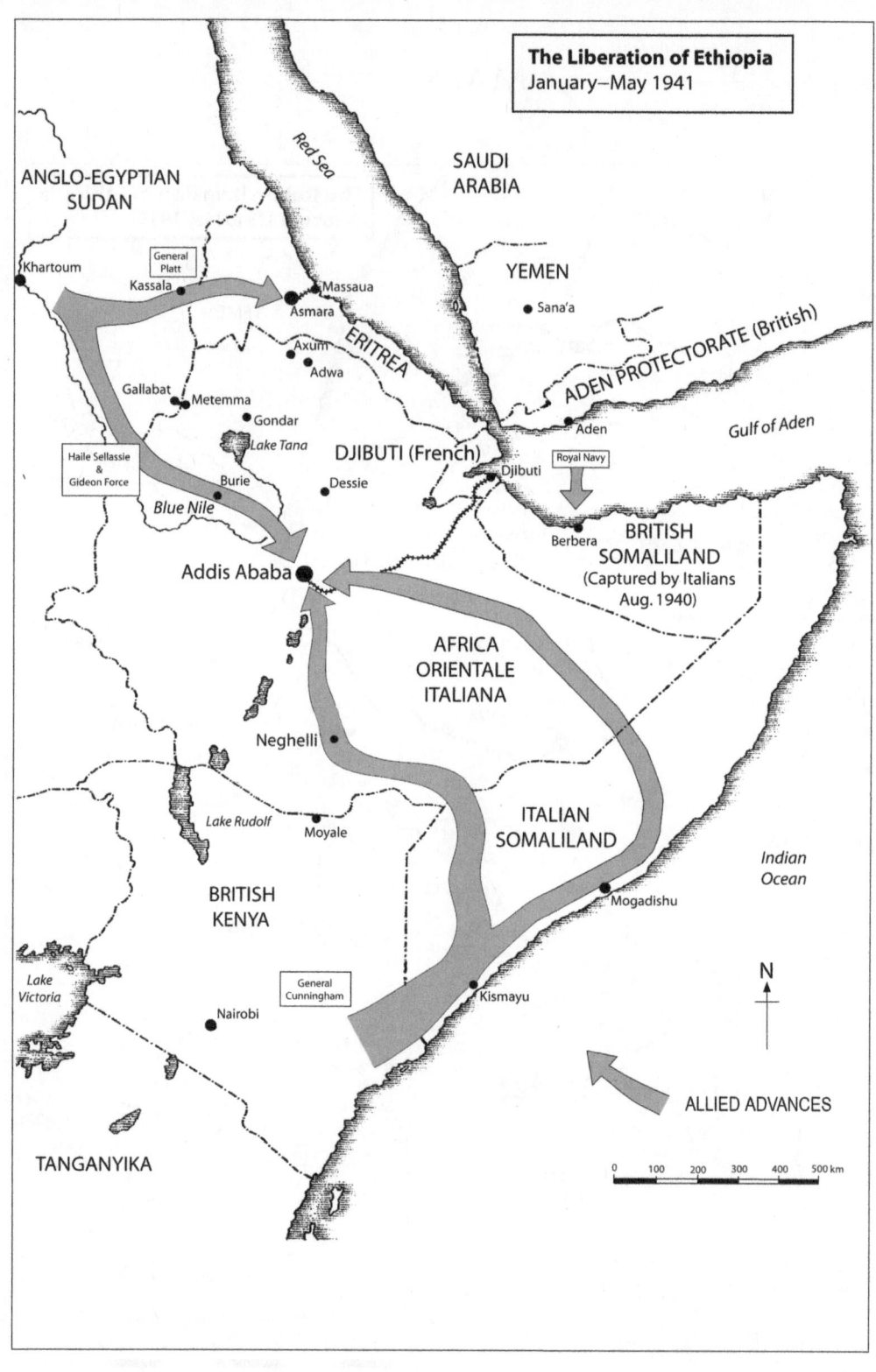

The Liberation of Ethiopia
January–May 1941

Red Sea

ANGLO-EGYPTIAN SUDAN

SAUDI ARABIA

YEMEN

Khartoum

General Platt

Kassala

Massaua

Asmara

Sana'a

ERITREA

ADEN PROTECTORATE (British)

Axum

Adwa

Gallabat

Metemma

Gondar

Aden

Gulf of Aden

Lake Tana

DJIBUTI (French)

Haile Sellassie & Gideon Force

Blue Nile

Burie

Dessie

Djibouti

Royal Navy

Berbera

BRITISH SOMALILAND
(Captured by Italians
Aug. 1940)

Addis Ababa

AFRICA ORIENTALE ITALIANA

Neghelli

Lake Rudolf

Moyale

ITALIAN SOMALILAND

Indian Ocean

BRITISH KENYA

Mogadishu

Lake Victoria

Nairobi

General Cunningham

Kismayu

N

TANGANYIKA

0 100 200 300 400 500 km

ALLIED ADVANCES

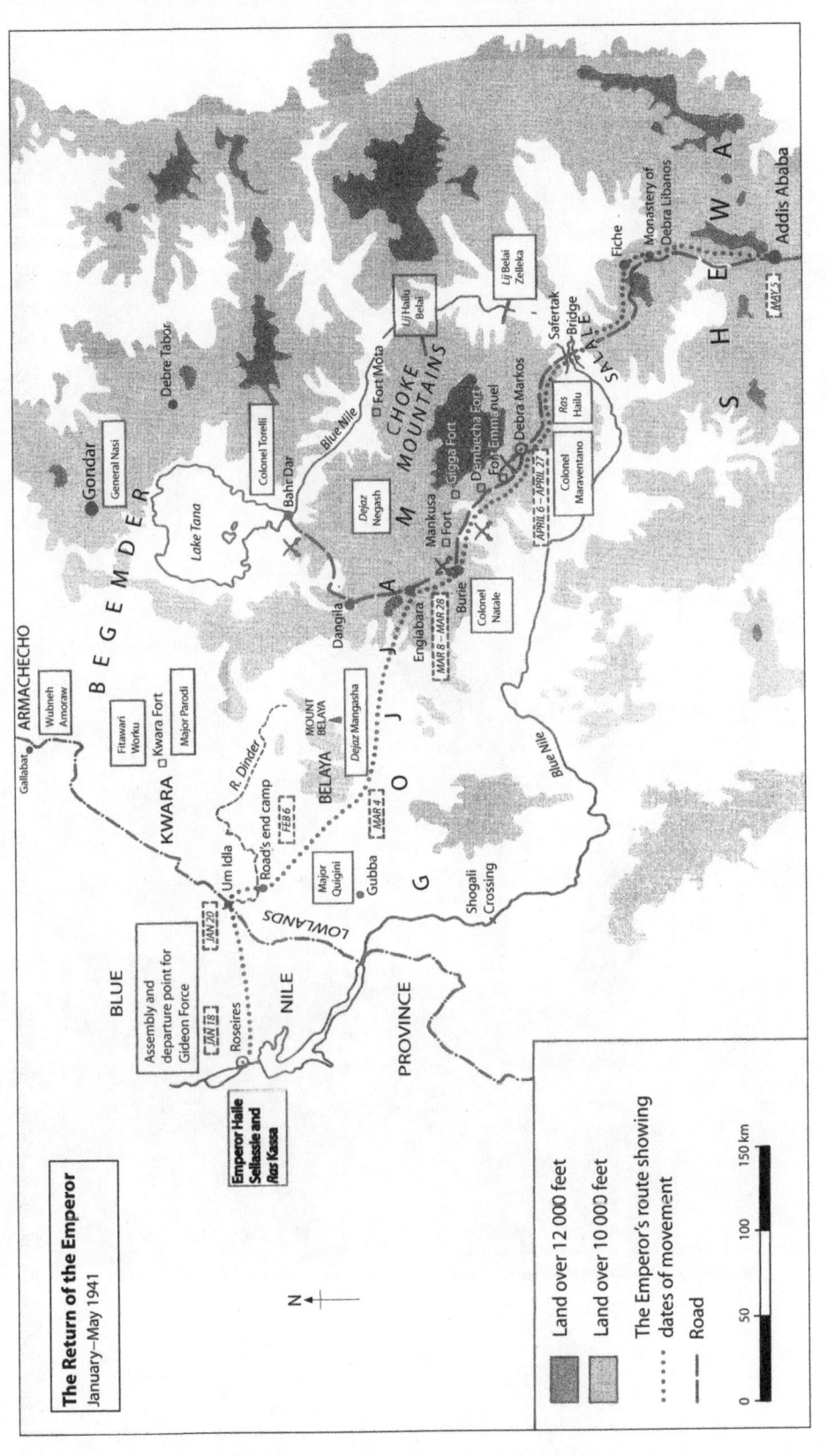

The Return of the Emperor
January–May 1941

N

Land over 12 000 feet

Land over 10 000 feet

The Emperor's route showing
dates of movement

Road

0   50   100   150 km

ARMACHECHO

Gallabat

Wubneh
Amoraw

BEGEMDER

Gondar

General Nasi

Debre Tabor

Lake Tana

Fitawari
Worku

Kwara Fort

Major Paradi

KWARA

R. Dinder

BELAYA

MOUNT
BELAYA

Dejaz Mangasha

Um Idla

Road's end camp

[FEB 6]

Major Quigini

Gubba

[MAR 4]

[JAN 20]

BLUE

Assembly and
departure point for
Gideon Force

Roseires

[JAN 18]

**Emperor Haile
Sellassie and
Ras Kassa**

NILE

PROVINCE

LOWLANDS

Shogali
Crossing

G   O   J

Blue Nile

Dangila

A   M

Englabara

[MAR 8 – MAR 26]

Burie

Colonel Natale

Colonel Torelli

Bahi Dar

Blue Nile

Fort Mota

Dejaz
Negash

Mankusa

Gigga Fort

Fort
Dembecha

Fort Emmanuel

Debra Markos

Colonel
Maraventano

[APRIL 6 – APRIL 27]

CHOKE
MOUNTAINS

Lij Hailu
Belai

Lij Belai
Zeleka

Safertak
Bridge

Ras
Hailu

S   A   L   L   E

Fiche

Monastery of
Debra Libanos

S   H   E   W   A

Addis Ababa

[MAY 5]

1

'BE CAREFUL NOT TO FORGET US'

Dejazmach Takla-Maryam Abayere

My name is *Dejazmach*[1] Takla-Maryam Abayere. I was born in
Shawa, Dabra-Berhan *awraja* [sub-province] at a place known as
Enawari. The date was 27 June 1915. My mother died when I was
two years old and my father when I was eight. It was therefore my
elder brother who brought me up, taking me to join him where he
was living near Harar. At Qarsa, I was employed as a boy soldier
at the age of ten, according to the tradition of a foster home.

In 1929, after I completed my church education at the church
of Giyorgis at Qarsa, some distance west of Harar, we learnt
that Italian forces had penetrated Ethiopian territory in the
Ogaden. *Dejach* Gabra-Maryam [Gari] was, in the meantime,
ordered to lead the army of Harar to fight the intruding Italians.
All my brothers, namely Ratta, Ashene and Malaku, travelled
with the army, since they were soldiers, but I was told to remain
at home as I was under age. At the time I was fourteen years old.

Fortunately, I was allowed to accompany the army as far as
a place called Elgobaya to see my brothers off. There, *Dejach*
Gabra-Maryam prepared a small feast, and three days later
gave an order for the retinue to turn back, and for anyone who
was not recruited not to remain with him. At this juncture,
all those who had come to accompany the army turned back,
but I hid myself there and later on joined the army and my

brothers. From Elgobaya we travelled for thirty-four days until we reached the Ogaden.

On our arrival, however, we could not find the Italians. They had already withdrawn to their territory, Italian Somaliland, from Qalafo (which was more than a kilometre within our territory), having been informed about our march. *Dejach* Gabra-Maryam then assigned three units as frontier garrisons, each having 300 soldiers: the first unit at Ogaden Wabi Shaballe was under *Grazmach* Tafara Balachew (nicknamed 'Lion of the Ogaden'), the second at Danane was under *Grazmach* Ababa and the third was under a certain *Balambaras*. The rest of us returned to Harar with *Dejach* Gabro-Maryam.

The Italians continued to cross the frontier on occasions. In 1932, as their forces had inflicted an attack upon our small forces near the border, *Fitawrari* Wagayahu was sent to the area. He was wounded in a minor clash and later died. As a result, a number of military missions were sent to the area to prevent recurring Italian assaults.

In 1934 [December] *Fitawrari* Alamayahu Goshu was sent to Wal Wal with his large army. This was the first incident in which the Italians had sent a large armed force. The previous trivial border skirmishes now led to fierce fighting in which the Italians killed many of our soldiers. On their side, too, a large number of soldiers died. The leader of our force, *Fitawrari* Alamayahu, was also killed in the action.

After the incident at Wal Wal we confronted the enemy at Qorahe and Dagahabur as it advanced following the invasion proper[2] [in October 1935]. At Dagahabur three tanks were captured and later brought to the town of Jijiga, driven by the Emperor's chauffeur *Grazmach* Umar, who was called from Addis Ababa for this purpose. After this, His Majesty himself came to Jijiga and inspected the tanks, and was then flown to Dire Dawa. The Italians tried to attack the Emperor's 'plane, but their attempt was futile.

After returning to Addis Ababa, His Imperial Majesty marched to the north and fought the Italian main force. The result was, however, defeat [at Maychew] and on 4 April 1936, the Ethiopian army was completely routed after which the Emperor retreated to Addis Ababa. Following his return to the capital, his intention was to continue his struggle by ambushing and fighting the enemy up to death. But the *Abuna* [Archbishop] and his *Mekwanent*[3] pleaded that 'It would be better if you go abroad and appeal to the League of Nations, for it is of no value if you die [fighting].' Thus he set off for Dire Dawa.

Until the defeat of the Emperor's army in the north, our force in the east had not been broken through. But as news of the Emperor's defeat on the northern front was heard we became demoralised and retreated from Dagahabour. After a while, however, we decided that we had to turn back and put up a stronger resistance. For this purpose I was given ten men with whom I hunted down our own soldiers who were retreating or deserting due to loss of morale.

Before he left Addis Ababa for Dire Dawa, His Imperial Majesty had *Dejach* Nasibu Za'amanuel, *Dejach* Ababa Damtaw, *Dejach* Made Habta Sellasie and *Dejach* Makonnen Endalkachew called back from the Ogaden, where they were campaigning. At Dire Dawa, after he met these noblemen, the Emperor made an unforgettable speech. He said:

> We shall return after three months, three years, or even five years. Those of you who are capable, wait for us, fighting in the bush and valleys. Those of you who are not capable, nevertheless be careful not to forget us, for when we return, we will have our revenge if you have collaborated with the Italians!

Balambaras Berhane-Masqal, *Kegnazmach* Tadla, *Kegnazmach* Makuriya Bantyirgu, *Ato* Zallaqa and others accompanied the Emperor and his entourage down to Djibouti and then returned, calling into Dire Dawa on the way back, while the other important officials went abroad with the Emperor.

After the Emperor's flight, all the forces from Harar and the surrounding areas that had returned from the Ogaden began their Patriotic struggle. Like my brothers, I became a Patriot.

Early in the month of May, the advancing Italians had garrisoned a division around Qulebi. To stop the passage of this force to Shawa and Addis Ababa, we surrounded the area and closed the road, denying the enemy any movement. *Fitawrari* Ba'eda Gabre then joined us in the chain of hills of Mount Garamulata where we had fortified our positions against the enemy garrisons. Returning from the Ogaden campaign he had fought the Italians for about three months at Gursum, a few kilometres to the east of Harar, where he was Governor. Later, since the area was small and not favourable for ambushing, he stopped fighting there and came to where we were with his father, *Dejazmach* Gabre, who, although old and weak, fought beside us. On his arrival at Garamulata and Golla, we chose him to be our commander since he had the highest title among us, that of *Fitawrari*.

From the beginning of May 1936 onwards, we fought major battles at Yabat, and Warabele. The latter was the fiercest and we lost men like *Dejazmach* Tadassa, *Ato* Zallaqa and *Dejach* Tashoma Balata, and two others. We fought at Sanqalle as well. We had twenty-three major engagements before we were finally pushed back from our position in front of the enemy garrison at Qulebi, on 29 October.

The enemy forces had superior arms and were far more organised than we were, so that they eventually succeeded in breaking our lines. It was largely because of the strategic position we had taken that we had been able to inflict strong attacks on the enemy so far.

I remember one day that some forty men, including me, ambushed an enemy patrol close to their camp, on the orders of my brother Ashene (who was a member of the Imperial

Bodyguard). Further away in the camp itself, we could see a tent lit up by a mantle inside and appearing to us like a charcoal glow. We loaded our rifles with five bullets each and the machine-gunner with twenty, and aimed at the tent. When our leader counted up to three, we showered our bullets on the tent, as we were told to do just after he said '... three!'

The idea was to surprise the enemy, but by chance we killed six Italian Generals, four subordinates, and one *banda*[4] officer. We didn't know this at the time, only God did. But early the following morning, a certain *Ato* Ayala Karra told us what we had done. In fact, he also informed us that the enemy was preparing for a reprisal air raid. Fortunately, except for some enemy fire from the camp half an hour after our raid, we were not attacked during the night.

Afterwards, however, the enemy increased their forces and enrolled many more irregular troops, including *Amharas*. These irregulars were as knowledgeable as we were, and knew the land and our resistance tactics. With this, therefore, the confrontation became more or less a civil war. The enemy, with their help, began to inflict severe attacks on us with their numerous and mobile cannons, and on 29 October we lost our position and retreated, as we could no longer hold on.

Having abandoned our fortifications near Qulebi, we retreated further south-west to the Jaja and Jarjartu areas in Chercher. At Jarjartu the enemy encircled us from two directions and for three days a violent fight took place. We had some initial success, but, owing to their strong support, they were able to force us to withdraw from this area as well.

We didn't do any more fighting in Haraghe province after that. Instead, we began our march to the neighbouring province of Bale in order to join forces with His Excellency, *Ras* Dasta Damtaw, *Dejazmach* Gabra-Maryam, *Dejazmach* Bayana Mar'ed, *Fitawrari* Shimeles [Habte] and Princess Romana Warq [Mangasha].[5] After a long march we reached

Bale in March 1937, but unfortunately we failed to meet up with them as they had already moved north to attack the enemy around Addis Ababa under the command of *Ras* Dasta, though the remnants of them later fled to Kenya.

Only Major [later General] Asfaw Walda-Giyorgis was left in Bale with some forty soldiers and two machine-guns. It was he who told us that *Ras* Dasta and the others had left for Shawa. Thanks to the shrewd nature of our supreme leader, *Fitawrari* Ba'eda, who immediately sent two men to see how *Ras* Dasta and his forces were going to Shawa (for a reward of a rifle and a hundred *Birr*[6] each) we were able to discover that *Ras* Dasta had been captured by the enemy and executed. The messengers also told us that all the important figures that were with the *Ras* had been summarily killed by the enemy, except for the Princess, who had been taken prisoner.

We now came to the understanding that we could not go anywhere as we had previously planned. With *Fitawrari* Ba'eda as the head, we convened a conference among the leaders. I had been granted the title of *Grazmach* in the struggle (through the traditional process of electing distinguished members by the rest of the group). So I was also to attend the meeting, during which it was decided that we must go back to Hararghe. A count of our number had been carried out shortly before the meeting, and we discovered that we were well over 17,000 in number.

Before we left Bale, the enemy advanced from Arusi province and attacked us from across the Wabe River. We were at a hill called Golocha, where we had found a very big cannon with twelve cannon balls, left behind by our forces owing to its heavy weight. When confronted with the enemy on the other bank of the river that separates Bale and Arusi, a certain blacksmith named Gabre said, 'If you can get this cannon up the hill, I will fire it.' So, with eight oxen drawing it, we dragged the cannon to the hilltop, after which the blacksmith fired all twelve cannon balls at the enemy. With their smaller cannons

firing with a far shorter range, the enemy forces were soon devastated and lost much of their baggage. After this we pushed
the cannon down the hill and moved north-east to Hararghe.
Meanwhile, the Italians showered us with bombs from their
aeroplanes in reprisal and killed so many of our men that we
couldn't collect the dead. On their side, two planes were shot
down by our forces. One of the flying officers was alive, having survived the crash, and so we captured him and took him
with us to the Ethio–Somali border.

However, we could not completely resist the enemy, and so
we had no alternative but to go back the way we had come.
While at Jarjartu, *Fitawrari* Ba'eda issued an order. It permit-
ted those of us who could not travel the difficult journey to join
Kegnazmach Lule, a Patriot who, after being captured by the
Italians, had become a *banda*. In granting them this freedom,
Fitawrari Ba'eda meant that they should collaborate with the
Italians so as to avoid further suffering, rather than compelling
them to continue as Patriots willy-nilly. On the other hand, he
also ordered those of us who had the strength and the will to
continue with him. As a result, about 13,000 joined the Lule
banda, and only around 4,000 remained with *Fitawrari* Ba'eda
for the next move. One of the latter group was me.

Under our leader the rest of us who had opted to continue
started our journey across Fadis, Bakalisa and the Issa desert,
all the way to the British coastal fort at Berbera, in British
Somaliland. It was on 12 May 1937, after a five-day journey, that we reached it. On our arrival, *Ato* [later *Bitwaded*]
Zawde Gabra-Hiywot, who had fled there earlier with his 300
men, received us with the British officials there.

For the next three years we stayed there in the safety of
exile. But after this, the Italians entered the European war in
June 1940, following which they occupied Berbera, and we
were obliged to move to Kenya with the British. In Kenya,
the British formed an Ethiopian unit from us, as part of the

Regular Army, commanded by a British [actually South African] officer whose name was Colonel Kern. We were first trained in a modern way under Zawde as our Captain. I was appointed Corporal. Later, under Colonel Kern's command, we fought as part of the 2nd Division Liberation Force led by General [Alan] Cunningham that advanced from Kenya.

The British forces shed their blood on the battlefields just as one would do for one's own country. Also, they did not boast about any of their qualities. In the years of our exile they had taught us military parades, the tactics of modern warfare, etc., and so, during the campaign, we often went with some of them close to the enemy forts for reconnaissance. They would then make rough sketch maps and later bomb the enemy camp very precisely with their 'planes. They were, in short, very good at tactics.

In the Borana area, in the province of Sidamo, we fought the enemy and captured their fort at Erjiku. We also pushed them back at Surpa after a strong engagement in which one enemy general, twenty-four officers and 8,000 troops were captured. After this, our column was ordered to continue liberating Sidamo, where we, the main unit of Cunningham's force, advanced to the capital, Addis Ababa [via Harar] and entered it [a month] earlier than the Emperor.

Our main force entered Addis Ababa on 12 August 1941 and was stationed at Sidest Kilo.[7] Later that day *Balambaras* Berhana-Masqal led us to the Palace where His Majesty received us. He said to us 'Congratulations on your repatriation to your country!' And thanks to our training in modern military discipline and our fine uniforms, we saluted him smartly.

The Emperor then decreed, 'Do not say, this is a *banda*, or this a refugee, or this a Patriot.' He added 'All are ours. It was Italy that defeated our country and captured it; Ethiopians did not willingly desert and join the Italians.' He concluded 'But we shall pay to each according to his works.'

We were, after this, invited to attend a feast and were given awards of cash. In the later days some of us joined the Imperial Bodyguard while others joined the regular Ethiopian Army.

With the rank of Sergeant I then headed to Dasse to serve His Majesty's heir, Crown Prince Asfa Wossen, with some men under me. After this I continued to serve in the military up to securing the rank of Colonel. By 1962, I was Governor-General of two different *awraja* [sub-provinces] and for this I earned the title of *Dejazmach*, of which I am very proud. Owing to my contributions during all those years I have been awarded the medals you see in my picture.

NOTES

1. For a list of military titles see Notes on Titles in the Glossary.
2. The Wal Wal Incident occurred in December 1934 wherein a remote Ethiopian military post on the disputed Italian Somaliland border region was attacked by Italian troops. It was the first harbinger of the war which was to follow.
3. *Mekwanent*, Nobleman, normally a rank obtained by merit or service.
4. *Banda*, or *Bande*, the Italian term for a group or band of soldiers, and by extension in the Ethiopian context, irregular or 'native' troops in Italian service.
5. Romana Work, a daughter of Emperor Haile Sellassie born before his marriage to Empress Menen, and prior to their imperial coronation, was not therefore officially regarded as a Princess. She was married to a prominent courtier and military commander, *Dejazmach* Bayana Mar'ed, who was killed by the Italians in February 1937. She was subsequently taken as a prisoner to Italy, and died there in 1941.
6. *Birr*, literally in Amharic 'silver', the name given to the silver currency introduced by Emperor Menelik in 1894, and later reintroduced by Haile Sellassie. See Richard Pankhurst, *Economic History of Ethiopia 1800–1935,* Addis Ababa (1968) pp. 460–94.
7. The term Sidest Kilo refers to the intersection of '*sidest*', or six, roads by Haile Sellassie's Palace (now Addis Ababa University's central campus), and by extension to the Palace itself.

2

'WE THOUGHT WE WOULD PUSH THEM BACK TO ERITREA'

Kenyazmach Woreda Kassa

Kenyazmach Woreda Kassa is my full name. I belong to the Tigre ethnic group and am now eighty-two. It was near the town of Adawa, in Tigray, that I was born and later, when Italy invaded our country, that I joined the resistance force under my immediate commander, *Dejazmach* Abbay Kahsay. I then went with my commander to the Ethio–Eritrean frontier, along the Mareb River, to join the forces commanded by *Le'ul Ras* Seyoum, who was the supreme commander of the forces in the region.

My family had a history of military service. My father was a soldier as well as a church man, and I was brought up with close connection to the [provincial] palace. Whether we were sent to school, or engaged in farming, we were destined finally to become members of the military. Our father had thirty or forty rifles, and we were given some of these and sent out with servants to train by shooting wild fowl. My father himself used to train and encourage me to master shooting. He instructed me to shoot at targets hung on tree trunks and would shout, 'Make your arm strong!' Whenever I missed the target, he would punish me. In such a way, he taught me to shoot well, standing as well as kneeling. I was able to practice by buying bullets and making *kilis*.[1]

After our advance to the Mareb following the Italian invasion we fought a lot and many of us died. Among those who lost their lives were *Fitawrari* Asefa, *Kegnazmach* Gebre-Egziabhare, *Dejazmach* Gebra-Heywot, *Dejazmach* Sahle, and *Dejazmach* Abbay. After that we returned to Adwa and from there we were called to Tembein to be close to the Emperor's force. Through Mayknetar and War'e we crossed to Tembein and were stationed in the small desert called Work Amba. We were fighting throughout the whole journey up until January 1936.

While we were in Tembein, *Ras* Kassa [Hailu] came leading an army from Shewa. Later, when the Emperor came to Maychew,[2] he called us, saying, 'Come here, leave Tembein. Let us be together!' So we moved to Maychew across Sehert, Maina'edin and Mai'agem. There, the Emperor had taken up position and he had fortified it well. While the leaders met the Emperor, the rest of us took up the positions assigned to us, and made fortifications.

In the months of January and February, 1936, the enemy dropped explosives called geletina upon our forces, killing many animals and causing immense destruction of material. They had been doing this ever since the first fighting along the Mareb. In addition, they showered mustard gas[3] just like rain. This poison affected horses, mules and people alike, and by burning up their bodies would finally claim their lives. As a result, the battle became very difficult for us. The poison made people victims of an incurable disease. Nonetheless, enduring all this, they never refused to fight.

The first weapon we had was the Senadir.[4] Later we got the long and short Wechefo and Leben rifles. Eventually, His Majesty brought and gave us Belgig rifles. We had no wireless sets and had to communicate by conveying letters by messengers who would have to travel for a week or two on foot or horseback to transport the mail.

At first we hoped to contain the Italian advance at the Mareb as we had a strong force, and we were well armed with swords, Wechefos, Lebens, Mausers and even some machine-guns. We were confident to the extent that we thought we would push them back to Eritrea, saying to ourselves, 'We will enter Asmara by smashing this Italian force!' What changed our thinking, and forced us to retreat, was the bombing and the mustard gas that they showered upon us. It was this that forced us to retreat from the Mareb to Tembein, and later to Maychew, where we lost the battle (but not the war).

Many members of the army, and even the Imperial Bodyguard, were killed. Many *Dejazmach*s also lost their lives, charging into the midst of the battle chanting inspirational war songs. At last, His Majesty decreed: 'Well! I have lost many people. I will present a petition to the League of Nations, for I am not going to lose the rest. But you who remain, never sub-mit to being ruled by another country. Use whatever weapons you have to hand. I will come back soon.'

After this decree, as Patriots, we followed our commanders as they dispersed to Tigray, Gondar and Wello. With my com-mander, I too moved to the Telemt-Gondar area, from where we travelled along the War'e River gorge and across to our home country of Tigray. While we were doing this we were able to carry out rigorous spying on the enemy, who was pre-occupied with clearing roads. However, some worthless fellow country-folk caused us trouble by telling the enemy where we were. Thus, we stayed for some time in our home country – Adwa, Shire, and near Mareb – fleeing to the Telemt in times of danger. We spent such a terrible routine of struggle until the day finally came when the Emperor returned.

His Majesty returned through Omedla to Gojjam. Where we were, we first heard about it from the flying papers[5] dropped by an aeroplane, bearing the headline 'The Conquering Lion of Judah, an Elect of God'.[6] From these papers we were able to know what was going on. Later, we heard people say that the Emperor had come to visit and give us rifles and information. Previously, before his return, the Emperor had sent us money through Metema while he was in the Sudan and we got three or five *Birr* each, on different occasions.

The kind of fighting we adopted was determined according to the different conditions. Sometimes, when the enemy came well armed, we waited until we were better equipped ourselves. We fortified positions under the cover of precipices controlling water sources and shot the enemy's horses and mules as they came to drink. On the other hand, if they came guided by *bandas* who knew the area, we would quickly retreat. This was how we fought.

Generally speaking, we used to rout and weaken the enemy, and we were seldom weakened by them. We captured their forces, plundered their guns and bandoliers, and sent their officers back empty handed. They took no rifles and machine-guns from us; Ha! Ha! How the brave people of Ethiopia sent them back empty handed! What did I look like? When the enemy surrendered I was just twenty-one, though I had a big clump of hair.[7]

From my time as a Patriot, the battles of Tembein, Abby Ado and Mareb are ones I will never forget. Once, *Dejazmach* Abbay Kashsau-Abay Gemora – 'Volcano' as we called him – captured eight large machine-guns, sixteen more of another kind, thirty automatic rifles, a number of strong mules (which the Italians called *fermo*) with their baggage, and 260 prisoners, all in one day! Having performed this feat, he equipped us with the captured weapons and, with our assistance, took the prisoners and handed them over to *Le'ul Ras* Seyoum.

After this, some forty Eritreans who had previously been fighting with the Italians surrendered to *Dejach* Abbay, and, begging him not to take away their arms, joined his forces. They then became our guides on our way down to the Mareb, showing us the enemy locations and forts. What's more, they

showed us where the Italians had buried boxes of hand grenades, which we dug up, and carried off on the *fermo* mules.

On my part, though the deeds I performed are not so great, I
remember one time at Limalimo, where we had moved to fight
against General Nasi, who had continued to fight in Gondar
after the Emperor's return. Before he submitted in November,
1941, we had to put up a hard fight against him in August.
At the end of that summer we were engaged in fierce fighting
with the Italians in the mountainous terrain of Limalimo. In
this the British assisted us by supplying provisions of salted
bread, sugar and tea. Once, there was a heavy rain that created a flood. The Italian forces were firing through the small
windows in their forts. While frantically running to escape the
heavy rain I saw Italian soldiers, wearing canvas capes, next
to their big machine gun which was loaded and ready to fire.
So, I threw a hand grenade and then made my escape. When,
after three days, our forces reached the area, we found three
dead Italian soldiers lying on the ground next to their machine
gun. For this, my commanding officer awarded me the highly
prized Medal of St George.

This was not the only time. Every time I went out to the ene-
my-held areas I never returned without bringing back a mule
or a horse. I seldom went into any of the villages in these areas,
though once, by disguising myself, I entered a village where
there was a feast and enabled my fellow Patriots to take what
we could back to the bush.

The northern part of the country is mostly mountainous.
However, what we most often held were the gorges, and we
posted some of our men to watch and stand ready at the cliffs.
Whenever necessary, we went up to the top of the adjacent
hills, carried out raids, and then got back to the gorges again.
From there, we quickly moved to other places in order to avoid
being attacked. Previously, a Belgian military mission had
come and given military training to the leaders of our forces,

teaching them not to cluster together when the enemy came. They also taught them not to wait for an aircraft by staying in one place, but to scatter and then stand still, hiding their rifles so that they would look like trees. We too learnt these tactics and applied them.

Frankly speaking, in all the areas of my Patriotic struggle, the peasants were Patriots as well. Had the peasantry not assisted, fed and hosted us, we would not have been able to survive those times. The peasants were the true Patriots. For this reason, I thank them; my appreciation goes beyond bounds.

My contemporary fellow Patriots and I, under our commanders, had good contacts with the Patriots in Tigray, Gondar (especially Telemt) and Sekota. Leaders such as *Dejazmach* Admasu and *Dejazmach* Wesen Hailu from Sekota, *Dejazmach* Dagne and *Dejazmach* Breaded from Belesa, *Dejazmach* Negash Worknch from Semein, *Dejazmach* Tiruneh from Telemt, as well as *Dejazmach* Adane and *Dejazmach* Yehualaneh from Welkait, all had contact with our leaders *Dejazmach* Abbay Kahsay, *Dejazmach* Gebre Meshesha, *Dejazmach* Sahle and *Dejazmach* Mesfin. We sometimes even went to these neighbouring leaders and stayed up to a week with them consulting one another. Other leaders did not wait for us to go to them, they came to the areas where we were stationed, and spent nights with us. The comradeship we shared was truly extraordinary.

The enemy fought while clearing roads. They used dynamite to blow up rocks, which we thought were explosives targeted against us! They used a large amount of explosives in cutting the mountain roads of Limalimo, Adi Gabre, and Boguna. They often moved with tanks and artillery; therefore, unless we caught up with them suddenly, they were unapproachable, especially since they also buried landmines in the surrounding area. The Italian forces eventually yielded only because the British came to our assistance.

The loosely woven garment we call *abujedid*[8] was what we commonly wore, though some might wear a uniform captured from the militia, or *banda*, or taken off dead enemy soldiers. We would take the clothes to the Tekkeze River and wash them clean before wearing them. We felt no shame. Sometimes, where the Italians retreated in a hurry leaving their tents, we took the canvas and made it into clothing.

When the Duke of Aosta fled following His Majesty's return, we moved to Amba Alage to capture him. *Le'ul Ras* Seyoum, at that time, broke into an Italian weapons depot and seized some 7,500 rifles, and, marching to Amba Alage through Sekota he completely devastated it. Assisted by the British in destroying enemy fortifications with artillery, we achieved an easy victory in three months. After this, we moved to Gondar under *Dejazmach* Gabra-Heywot and *Dejazmach* Abbay, as the Italian commander Nasi had refused to surrender. Many resistance leaders, including *Ras* Berru from Shewa and *Ras* Azana from Gondar, had to campaign against him as he fought on until November 1941, when at last victory was ours.

Coming back home – and to my birth place – just after the victory at Gondar, I found my father's big single-storey house and our beehive had been burnt to ashes. I was so disappointed about what had happened. So, I decided to take revenge and began to search for the ones who had done all this to my family's property. With the help of the three soldiers that I had earlier been given to lead by my father, I found the guilty villagers, burnt their houses in retaliation and then ran away from the area. Fleeing from the village where I was born and raised, and having been recognised by no-one, I went and joined the Ethiopian Army in a far away British camp.

From 1942 up until 1974 I served my country in the military. During my career as a soldier, there is no place in the country that I have not been. After I accomplished my duties, being dispatched to Dessie and Karrakore, with the Ethiopian Army in the British camp in Tigray, I rendered further military service between 1952 and 1960 in Eritrea. Under a UN mission, I was then sent to the Congo during the crisis, and stayed there for a year and three months. Following this, I was sent to the Ogaden region and served there for some seven years. I was also in Bale for three years. Having served the Imperial Government, moving from place to place like this, I was retired in 1974, after which I served as a respected local judge in my village in Addis.

As a result of the cruel actions of the enemy, a number of heroes died on our side. Foreigners took away the wives of our commanders, and their beautiful white or grey horses. Despite trying not to see it that way, I still have a great grievance about that. Whatever the case, the brave Ethiopians offered a heroic resistance, being inspired by the love of their country, freedom, and religion. This is what had prevailed in earlier times, during the reigns of Emperors Tewodros, Yohannes, and Menelik,[9] which should never be forgotten. How can what Emperor Tewodros achieved against the British at Magdala, what *Ras* Alula did in smashing the Italians [before the Fascist invasion] at Dogali and in presenting the glorious victory to his commander Emperor Yohannes, or what *Ras* Mengesha, *Ras* Alula Abba Negga and Emperor Menelik did in defeating Italy at Adwa,[10] ever be forgotten? We have ever since fought strongly to maintain this historical tradition, insisting, with God's help, on never surrendering.

Ethiopia is a nation that never yields to an invader and that never accepts foreign rule. The people do not want others' treasures; nor do they invade others' countries. But when someone comes against their country, they turn him back by dismembering the limbs of his forces, just like *Ras* Mengesha did at Adwa. The nation generally stands firm. The children of Ethiopia never say 'But I have a wife! or a family! or cattle!' They always defend their country and compatriots first of all.

Inspiring war-chants are our tradition, and we used to sing the following:

They have come against us,
And let us go as well,
They are not those lions,
But just men, like us.

The brave Patriot, poorly armed, joining his compatriots.
He is black, his leader's black, and his country's black,
He resembles a fierce satanic being.

For my part in the Patriotic struggle and my subsequent military service I was awarded twelve medals from the Emperor, at different times. These are: the Five Years' Patriotic Service Medal, the Star of Victory, the Cavalry Grade Medal, three golden and one silver Medal of Emperor Menelik, an Adventure Medal, the Memorial Medal of the Congo Campaign, the Ethiopian Star of Africa, the Val Medal of the Congo Veterans, and the Star of Africa (which I acquired at Limalimo in Gondar).

During their stay in Ethiopia the Italians constructed roads from Asmara to Addis Ababa, Addis Ababa to Jimma, as far as Gojjam, Sidama, and Harar. However, they were all made with the blood of us Ethiopians. True, they have constructed good roads, and established trade and industry; however, countless skilled labourers died in the process. It should also be noted that they built these roads for their own benefit. What does it profit us to have roads, whilst being slaughtered and robbed of our health and cattle, as well as raping our wives, during those five years? In fact, the roads have been beneficial for us since we liberated our country, but still, we will never forget the outrages of the enemy.

Finally, I advise this generation to maintain the love of its fathers and of its country. For my part, I am still ready to stand for my country and to obey the government. I even asked to campaign at Badime[11] when it was invaded [by Eritrea in May 1998]. What would happen to me? I can still fight by firing from fortifications. Yes, I am ready to stand and fight for my country as well as I can!

NOTES

1. *Kilis*, recycled bullets.
2. Maychew, or Mai Chaw, literally Salty Water, or River, was the site of the Emperor's defeat on the northern Front, at the end of March 1936. See Angelo Del Boca, *The Ethiopian War 1935-1941*, Chicago and London (1960), pp. 161–71.
3. For an extensive study of the Italian use of mustard gas see Angelo Del Boca, *I gas di Mussolini. Il fascismo e la guerra d'Etiopia*, Rome (1996).
4. For a description of the weapons in general use during this period see Note on Firearms.
5. i.e. leaflets. These were published weekly during the British campaign, and were dropped by the British Royal Air Force. They bore the heading 'Bandarachin – Our Flag', together with a representation of the Ethiopian Lion of Judah and stripes in the colours of the Ethiopian flag: green, yellow and red. On this Anglo-Ethiopian aerial propaganda, see George L. Steer, *Sealed and Delivered*, London (1942), pp. 90–101.
6. These were the titles adopted by the Emperor. On the history of the Lion of Symbol see Sven Rubenson, 'The Lion of Judah: Christian Symbol and/or Imperial Title' in *Journal of Ethiopian Studies* (1965) III no. 2, pp. 75–86.
7. The Patriots, who wore what might now be called an 'Afro' hairstyle, had vowed that they would not cut their hair until Ethiopia was liberated.
8. *Abujedid*, cheap cotton cloth, mainly imported from India.
9. *Kenyazmach* Worede is here referring to the wars of the three previous Emperors: Tewodros (reigned 1855–68), Yohannes (r.1872–89), and Menelik (r.1889–1913).
10. The reference is to Menelik's resounding victory over the Italians at the battle of Adwa in 1896 which preserved Ethiopian independence.
11. Ethiopia's northern most point near the disputed border with Eritrea.

3

'POISON HAS BEEN SHOWERED UPON US, AND OUR COUNTRY HAS BEEN DESPOILED'

Grazmach Hagos Hailu

My name is *Grazmach* Hagos Hailu. I am now eighty-three. I was born and raised in Adwa *awraja* (administrative district) Hamushte Zufan Endakatsahma *woreda* (sub-district). I am a Tigre-born.

All the Patriots in my area, including myself, were children of the *Naftegna*.[1] We had the *naft*s of our fathers at home. Soon after the enemy aggression, *Atse* [Emperor] Haile Sellassie issued a decree as King of Kings, with the message 'You Ethiopians! It is your national obligation! Stand-to and campaign like your forefathers. Observe your purpose and follow your leader!' This decree was announced accompanied by the beating of a *negaret* [war drum]. At the time my father was sick, so I picked up the Wechefo rifle we had at home and joined the local force led by my immediate commander *Kegnazmach* Kassa Gebrekidan, son of *Ras* Gebrekidan Bitwaded. Under his leadership, I went to Adwa and joined the standing army which had been raised under the supreme leadership of the area's governor *Le'ul Ras* Seyoum Mengesha.

Italy had at that time started a war of aggression on the Mareb front.[2] There were eight *Dejazmach*s to provide a defence. At Adwa a parade was held and inspiring war-chants were sung. The Ethiopian heroes chanted, 'We shall spend the night in Asmara, marching from Adwa', demonstrating their determination to accomplish their duty.

Following this, to herald the beginning of the war to Addis Ababa, a beacon made from a bunch of thin, dry branches was lit by the fortress keepers up there. This signal fire was visible to *Dejazmach* Ambachew's regional administrator, Semien, which was a three-day march away. On receiving the message, Semien passed it on to the next region. By so doing, the one receiving the signal and passing it on to the other, the news of the start of the war reached Addis Ababa in less than an hour! This was the start of the war by the eight *Dejazmach*s under *Le'ul Ras* Seyoum, as decreed by the Emperor. At the Mareb frontier were *Dejazmach*s Gebremedhin, Sahel, Belay and Abay Kahsay, and these were the four *Dejazmach*s who fired the opening shots.

In this situation where the whole of Ethiopia had arisen, a false message, disguised as the Emperor's order, reached *Le'ul Ras* Seyoum, commanding him to take the army back to Tembein. By virtue of this, all those *Dejazmach*s and the great army, which had been so proud to be energetically moving forward so that they could 'spend the night in Asmara', had to return to Tembein.

After the return of that great army to Tembein, the forces of another eight *Dejazmach*s came from Shewa, led by *Ras* Kassa Hailu, and joined them there. Hence, the forces of a total of sixteen *Dejazmach*s came under the supreme leadership of *Le'ul Ras* Seyoum, each establishing their own spheres of engagement and fortifying their positions to escape air raids.

The enemy forces, on the other hand, coming all the way from Asmara and passing through the defence line of the Mareb, from which we had earlier retreated, were happy to take control of Adwa. While the forces of *Ras* Kassa from Shewa were intact, some of the forces belonging to that area [northern Tigray] were ordered to go back into the interior parts of the Adwa *awraja*, such as Hamedo and Dahro Tehli, which the enemy had captured. This command was given to us by *Dejazmach* Abay [at that time *Fitawrari*] who forwarded it after discussing the decision with about thirty nobles close to him. So, we went back to the interior of Adwa *awraja*, to areas like Zengwi and Enda-Selassie. The Italians came under Marshal [Emilio] De Bono, and being much stronger with the help of *banda*s, we were forced to retreat to Tembein where, under the command of *Dejazmach* Abay, we once again merged with the force under *Le'ul Ras* Seyoum in order to attack the enemy and our deserter countrymen.

At Tembein, our forces fought against the enemy for about six months. On 20 January 1936, the day of the celebration of the miracle at Cana in Galilee, a great many fighters died following the showering of mustard gas by Italian aeroplanes. Surviving Patriots of the sixteen *Dejazmach*s who could still manage to fight went down to Maychew to join the Emperor who had come there via Dessie. Those who could not fled to Wag, Semein, and Begemder, as the gas had either destroyed their health, blinded them, or burned their legs. *Le'ul Ras* Seyoum and *Ras* Kassa headed to Maychew and joined the Emperor. But there too the Italians sent about fifty aeroplanes and routed our forces.

As for myself, I fled to Sekota with others, for I had had enough of the poison gas at Tembein. It smelled so hazardous and we were all disorientated, to the extent that we could hardly recognise our way for the three days it took to reach Sekota.

What we had been doing so far was accomplishing our national duty as soldiers. Patriotism began just afterwards. I became a Patriot when I refused to be ruled by the Italians who occupied the area after winning their temporary victory at Maychew. I joined the army of Begemder with the surviving force in Sekota. From Sekota to Lasta-Lalibela and Wag, everyone became a Patriot. And so I became part of the resistance in Begemder [Gayan, Debre Tabor, and Beleso], the land of folk heroes, and spent the next four years as a Patriot under my leader *Lij* Yohannes Iyasu,[3] who came from Wello.

Patriots used such guns as the Albin and Minishir which were taken as booty from the enemy. Before that, we fought with Wujigra, Wechefo, and the like. The nobles and the Army of the Imperial Bodyguard though had better and more modern weapons. Even the Emperor is said to have shot an aeroplane down with an Oerlicon [automatic machine-gun] while fighting at Maychew.

I fought for about a year in Tigray, including the battle at Tembein. I participated in the battle led and conducted by *Dejazmach* Hailu after I came to Sekota, and I was also at the battle of Ayne Baguna, in Lasta. After going to Begemder I took part in the engagement at Belesa and was wounded, shot in my right arm, in February 1938. These were the major events of my struggle during the four years that followed Tembein. The sum total would mean five years. During my time as a Patriot in Belesa and Gondar, my commander had become *Lij* Yohannes.

Inter-Patriotic ties among different regions were close. For instance, we used to give weapons to one another. Patriots of Showa, Gojjam and Begemder used to get the Albin rifle easily from the *banda*s and others in Wollo where they were abundant. They were sold for 300 *Birr* each. In addition to this, there was a high level of intelligence activity and everyone usually knew what number of Patriots there was after the fighting in Gojjam, Shewa, or Tigray, by exchanging information secretly, so we knew the quantity of weapons each region had. This intelligence was detrimental to the enemy. In general, on foot, on mule-back, or whatever means of transportation they travelled, the Patriots had a close relationship among themselves.

There was also a special relationship between the Patriots and the peasants. The Patriots had no power to safeguard the peasants properly from enemy attack. So what we did was to give rocket signals to the peasants (sometimes a signal of shouts or shots too) to convey the message 'The enemy has come upon you, be careful not to be looted, slaughtered and eaten!' The peasants would then save themselves by quitting their ploughing and running away. At other times, when an engagement was to take place in their village, we warned them 'Go! Leave! A battle will take place here! And the time at which Patriots will come is not known to be in the day or at night, so, leave!' Those who had guns often joined us with Patriotic zeal, while others took all their property, and more, somewhere else. For all these reasons, the country people gave a warm reception to the Patriots. They used to give us whatever we wanted.

Patriots evaluated the strength of the enemy forces by referring to intelligence material or using other methods. Then we would fight the enemy as suited us best – face-to-face if manageable, during the day time if possible, or at night if not. The foreigners (the Italians) stationed in camps did not attack us; in fact they were mainly the ones who were suffering. It was the native *banda*s who caused us the most trouble, by spying on us and collaborating with the enemy. What is amazing is the number of *banda*s' wives who, collaborating willingly or unwillingly, were *Yewist Arbegnoch*,[4] and bravely brought us bullets in their pots when leaving the camp to fetch water.

Often we controlled mountainous areas so that the enemy found it difficult to climb them. A mountain was like an ally to us. We were not troubled in climbing them even though we were barefoot. Mountainous areas and the night-time were both very helpful to us. However, sometimes the enemy army came in such unbearable strength that we could not defeat them by fighting alone. In such cases, we were forced to devise other methods.

Once, around 9:00 or 10:00 in the evening, we burnt dry grass that we had gathered in different places and fired shots from every direction to confuse the enemy into thinking that we were there in large numbers. This, and getting false reports from the country-dwellers that we were numerous bandit groups, resulted in the enemy spending the whole night shooting, and hence firing his bullets in vain.

In the areas where I was involved, there was no wireless or other means of communication. We exchanged messages by travelling on foot. Our feet never yielded to thorns or other hazards. For this reason we were nicknamed 'the Bare Feet'. Travelling so fast, the Patriot reached whatever destination he was sent, be it Tigray, Gondar, Shoa, or any other area, turning a journey of, say, eight days into three. No native Ethiopian came disguised as messengers from other regions to spy on us. Even the *banda*s studied us openly and not as spies.

We didn't have the formal uniform of a soldier. Most of us wore the shorts called *fido*, which were introduced in 1935. Apart from this, we used to take the clothes of the Italians we captured and wore them. In this way, we dressed ourselves as we had no one to provide us with clothes. But this did not trouble us much. What we suffered from most was the shortage of food after the enemy captured areas in which we had been stationed, and set fire to the surrounding areas. This often forced us to migrate to another area, consuming whatever food was available.

It was in 1935 that the enemy aircraft inflicted an attack on us at Adwa prior to our retreat to Tembien. We had never seen an aeroplane before, nor heard its noise. We had only heard that in Addis Ababa there was an object that was driven in the air. When I first saw one at Adwa, with two other men, it was difficult to believe there was a human being inside, for it was flying in the air. Together with the shooting and its noise, we were so confused that we said 'But now it is the Creator who fights us.'

During the five years of the Patriotic struggle His Majesty was in England. But those five years there were not spent in vain. When His Majesty left the country he left the other leaders to serve the Patriotic cause while he went to appeal to the League of Nations [in Geneva] saying, 'Poison [mustard-gas] has been showered upon us, and our country has been despoiled by Italian soldiers.'

There were some *banda*s who spread rumours that the Emperor had fled the country. A Patriot would never say that. The Emperor had only left after saying to us:

Be patriots! I am willing to die here with you, for it is very difficult for me to leave after travelling eight hundred kilometres with you from Shewa to Maychew. But if you tell me to go, then you will be patriots, and I will go to the League of Nations to appeal for help.

After making such promises to great men such as *Le'ul Ras* Seyoum, *Ras* Kassa and the *Ichege*,[5] he was ready to leave.

Having ordered his leaders to 'Protect the country while I appeal to the League of Nations' the Emperor left for Djibouti, after which he sailed to England by warship.[6] In England, the Emperor lived in a house he had bought[7] without being dependent on the British government, and from there he went to the League of Nations to report Fascist Italy's unfair treatment of Ethiopia.

Yes, the world war broke out because of us, the attitude towards Ethiopia and the Emperor's outlook. When Mussolini, and of course Hitler, bought and sold a country, the League of Nations' members said nothing. Hitler had threatened all the members and no-one dared say to him 'Why do you buy? Why do you sell [a country]?'

After Italy's entry into the European war, the British became involved and flew the Emperor to Khartoum, after which he led the liberation campaign in Gojjam. We Patriots followed his orders to 'Open the attack'.

Following the death of Bilatten-geta Hiruy [Wolde Sclassie] in London, Bilatten-geta Loreso Ta'ezaz became Minister of Foreign Affairs. He soon came and reassured us saying, 'Do not surrender to be ruled [by Italy] for a World War will erupt. A second World War will soon break out!' He had with him the notice which read 'The coming of the Lion of Judah!' and the flag to assure us that he had been sent by the Emperor. It was through

Metema, Armacheo and Begemder that he came and encouraged the Patriots in the areas. This is why we call the Gondar region the centre of the Patriots, for it had foreign contacts via Khartoum.

After Mussolini's entry into the European war, the British sent a message to us with a recommendation, saying, 'The British are signatories to our treaty. Notice you Ethiopians that all whites are not the same even though they all appear white.' In my area of involvement there was an English officer called General Fox coordinating the area where the Ethiopian Army was being reorganised. Others, obviously, included Wingate, being the royal advisor; Cunningham, who came into Ethiopia via Harar; Sandford, a politician as well as a soldier; and General Platt, who advanced from the North. The Commander-in-Chief was Marshal Montgomery[8] who came to visit Ethiopia in late 1940. I was able to see him face-to-face on his visit then. The supreme leader who commanded all this was Mr Churchill, in whose honour a street has been named in Addis Ababa, like many others who were hon-oured by Haile Sellassie.

One thing I remember is what I did in Gondar when the Italian Viceroy of the region, called Nasi, continued to fight even after the Emperor's return. The Italian refused to surrender and played havoc for about eight months. I campaigned, together with fellow Patriots, under the leadership of Prince Asfewesen, the Emperor's heir. In November 1941 we besieged Nasi in the town of Gondar. However, the town was fenced with electrified barbed wire. I soon devised a plan. I brought some donkeys, drove them upon the fence and broke it down (which killed the donkeys). We were then able to enter Gondar and capture Fasil's Palace.[9]

Just like Nasi, the Duke d'Aosta, who was Viceroy of Ethiopia, continued to fight with his 120,000-strong army to the north. At the time, *Lu'el Ras* Seyoum had returned from imprisonment in Italy [1937–39] with other nobles, and had been appointed by the Italians, as a collaborator, in charge of northern Ethiopia. However, he later opted to fight against Italy and returned to being the main resistor of the enemy forces in the north. When the Duke d'Aosta refused to submit, Seyoum captured him at Amba Alage from where he took the Duke and the other prisoners to Asmara, leading with his man *Dejazmach* Abay Kahsay in front of the captives. I was not at Gondar at that time, but my father was there as he had fought and been wounded at Amba Alage.

All this shows that I was involved in the liberation struggle even after the Emperor returned. Also, after all the Italians were captured, I spent some time at Dessie under *Fitawrari* Tesemma Trgete, as we were organised to give support to the Prince. For these reasons, I was able to meet the Emperor in 1943, after we had achieved the end of enemy occupation of the whole country.

One immense historical asset we Ethiopians have is that we had traditional military titles with names in our own language. Terms like Lieutenant, Sergeant, etc. are secondary to us, as Ethiopia has its own military titles and organisation[10] ranging from *Ras* to *Balambaras*. Having our own military culture and traditions were very important to our morale and will to fight. It was part of our culture to sing war chants on the battlefield. This is what I used to chant:

A killer[11] in his childhood,
A defender of his faith,
A killer fleeing into one's *kebele*[12]
A servant of Tekel.[13]

As for myself, I secured my rank in 1944, after the end of the struggle, from the hands of the Emperor himself. It is the rank of *Grazmach*, which I secured after my father died. I also received the Star of Victory Medal.

The important thing in attesting the wisdom of our Emperor is his determination not to imprison our Ethiopian compatriots whom we had captured while they were fighting for Italy. He once declared, 'My compatriots were forced to fight for

Italy.' We even handed over our Italian captives to the British, and never imprisoned any black or white. Moreover, our forces sometimes accompanied captured Italians to Asmara. However, they still had a bid for an overseas empire. Hence we helped our Emperor from the start so that he was at last able to secure our frontiers as far as the Red Sea [Eritrea] in 1952. Accordingly, His Majesty was recognised to be the only legitimate leader of Ethiopia thanks to us Ethiopians who served our country first as Patriots and later by serving our Emperor. In so doing, we were able to regain our lost territory, celebrating in a ceremony attended by the Emperor at the former Mareb frontier.

For our people, Fascist Italy brought nothing but worsening poverty. The British at least imported their knowledge and skills; but the Italians did not even make clothes for our bodies. For this reason, they were expelled once and for all. Even when we entered Asmara with the Emperor in 1952, there were no factories established there. All they had done were things that were beneficial to themselves, saying 'Asmara Tse'ada' – a 'White Asmara'. The Italians had exploited the native Eritreans.

Of the British officers I knew well, Captain Mike was the other one (in addition to General Fox and others whose names I cannot remember right now). He helped us a lot by clearing the way of landmines when we were marching to liberate Gondar. When Gondar was liberated, our flag was hoisted and General Fox made a speech in English in the Emperor's presence expressing his happiness. By November 1941 we were almost completely liberated but Europe was not yet. Captain Mike then said to us: 'Congratulations! You Ethiopians are lucky. As for me, I will not be changing out of my uniform as I am going back to Europe, for the Fascists, Nazis and Japanese have not yet fallen.' Having said this, he said 'Good-bye!' to us and departed. Later we heard that he was killed fighting in Sicily, and were very sorry for that.

NOTES

1. *Naftegna*, much of southern Ethiopia had been occupied in the late nineteenth century by Emperor Menelik's soldiers. Possessing numerous *naft*s, or rifles, they became known as *Naftegna* and represented a local elite.

2. The Mareb River marked the frontier between the Italian colony of Eritrea to the North, and independent Ethiopia to the South.

3. *Lij* Yohannes Iyasu, son of Emperor Menelik's grandson *Lij* Iyasu, the former ruler of Ethiopia who had been deposed in 1916.

4. *Yewist Arbegnoch*, literally 'Inside Patriots', civilian supporters or spies who lived for the most part in Addis Ababa and other towns. They were not engaged in fighting, but helped the patriots significantly in various ways, notably by supplying them with arms and medicine.

5. *Ichege*, traditionally the Patriarch or Head of the Ethiopian Orthodox Church.

6. In fact by a British warship through the Suez Canal to Gibraltar, and thereafter by ordinary steamship to Britain.

7. This probably refers to 'Fairfield', the house in Bath, which he subsequently donated to the local council for use by the aged. It is now being used by the council to house ethnic minorities.

8. Field Marshall Bernard Montgomery who famously defeated Rommel in North Africa.

9. The Royal Enclosure lies at the heart of the city. It contains five castles plus ancillary buildings and connecting tunnels. The original castle was built by Emperor Fasilidas (or Fasil) around 1640 and is the most impressive. Some of the buildings were partially destroyed when the British bombed the Italian headquarters.

10. For a list of military titles see Notes on Titles in the Glossary.

11. In this context, a heroic fighter.

12. *Kebele*, local administrative district.

13. *Tekel*, the shortened version of Abba Tekel, the Emperor's horse name. Horse names or war-names were names adopted during the conflict, similar to the French *'nom de guerre'*.

4

'FROM THE BEGINNING WE FOUGHT BY AMBUSHING'

Kegnazmach Admasu Zeleke

My name is *Kegnazmach* Admasu Zeleke. Because there was no birth record in those days, I do not know my exact age, though I was told that I was born in 1923 and so it means that I am now eighty-one. I was born in northern Gondar, in the Chilga *awraja*, at the place particularly known to be the hunters' country, and I am an Amhara.

I was very young when, following the example of others, I began my life as a Patriot. In the spring of 1936 we started the resistance in our area following the order given to our commander (and my uncle) *Dejach* Bayyu Melkie, by the supreme leader of the region's forces *Ras* Wubneh Tessema, before he left for the Sudan. I was then a thirteen-year-old church student. Patriots in every locality waged their resistance under their respective commanders. The leader of the forces in our area was, as I said, my uncle *Dejach* Bayyu. Because I was so young and did not have a gun, I served as bodyguard to my uncle, carrying one of his rifles.

I did not have any military training before I became a Patriot, however, as our area was known for bravery in hunting, we all learned how to fire a gun by the age of seven. My great-grandfather was a distinguished hunter, and so were my grandfather and my father. From childhood, we learned how to swim, ride a horse, and fire a gun, just like learning the alphabet. People older than us held the gun for us while we learned to shoot at a piece of cattle skin hung on a tree trunk as a target. That is how it was in our locality where the people were renowned for hunting lions and elephants.

The weapons we used in our area at first were outdated guns, such as Wechefo, Wujigra, Moskob and Senadir. But later came the rifles we called the 'Belgig', imported by the Ethiopian government from Belgium when it realised that Italy was preparing for war. The other better rifle was the Albin, which people like my uncle were able to get from across the Sudanese border via Matamma. As my uncle also had another gun, it was me who carried his Albin – a rifle I was taught to fire and with which I was well acquainted. The Italians, by contrast, had cannons, machine-guns, tanks, and bombs, and occasionally, when the fighting was fierce, mustard gas.

In the area I was involved in as a Patriot, right from the beginning, we fought by ambushing. After the Italian army ordered the entire population to hand over their weapons, the inhabitants of my home country, and other lowlanders, pro-tested and fled into the bush and deserts. Therefore, unlike most of the highlanders who obeyed the enemy, we of the low-lying plains opted for rebellion. The struggle between the enemy forces and our own was, therefore, characterised from the start by our forces first retreating and then chasing after the enemy. But later, as people began to understand guerrilla fighting, and as those who had deserted to the enemy came back to us and gave us their support, we started a stronger counter-offensive.

The peasants of the plain of Dembia collaborated with our Patriotic forces and put up a wonderful struggle. They had at first had to hand over their guns to the enemy, as they had many cattle and much wealth and they could not afford to abandon their productive plains. Afterwards, however, they cooperated with us. They gave us one *Birr* per household to buy ourselves trousers, and in return we guarded their cattle from thieves. Moreover, they never disclosed our position to the enemy. This made the area an important site for the Patriots, who were able to make it through to victory, enduring the drought that had prevailed in our areas following crop failures and invasions of locusts. During the famine, we were forced to eat wild animals and roots. But our Patriot forces couldn't have survived without the support of the highland people of Dembia and Wegera who offered us their cattle and stood by us.

Constantly fighting the enemy, we had fierce engagements at eighteen different places. These were tough battles which involved encircling the enemy and then attacking aggressively. The Italians fought with regular troops and *bandas*, who collaborated with them for various reasons – those who deserted the country forces were given pay, military uniforms and weapons to fight with.

Ours was not the only area of strong Patriotic resistance. The entire Begemder, northern Gondar – comprising Chilga, Armacheho, Quara, Wolkait Tegedie, Janora, Belesa, and Gaynt – was full of Patriots. The Italians captured only the towns and roads. Even the roads, towards the end, fell under our control through our ambushes. The enemy was confined to the towns, and dared not go out into the countryside. It was by ambushes and surprise attacks that we were able to capture so many guns.

One unforgettable and wonderful adventure I can speak about with pride is one in which I captured a number of guns. Obviously, a man who has not captured a weapon and has not performed a dangerous task is not a man. For this reason, in November 1939, I spent the whole day with a Muslim comrade called Mensur Ali spying on some Italians who were constructing a road. There were a number of civilian labourers as well as military personnel protected by three tanks. At about eight o'clock in the evening we went into their temporary camp. The Italians were having their supper in a shack made of tin sheets. Next to it was an empty tent which I crept into and seized two Albin rifles, two hand grenades and some cartridges. On coming out of the tent, I threw the grenades into the crowd of Italians who were eating their meal and ran away with my friend. I did not look back to see how many Italians were killed; I could only hear people shouting. In the meantime, someone guarding the camp from a nearby cliff began shooting at my friend and me. Anyway, we managed to escape and disappeared into the bush by rolling down the hill.

In our rush to avoid being hit, my friend and I were not able to escape together, and an instant later we had lost sight of each other. I assumed that he was killed somewhere in those bushes. Marching a distance of about thirty-five kilometres, I was able to get back to my village that night. A few days later we heard from people who had come from that area that I had killed many Italians and *banda*s. For this daring and aggressive action, I was given the nickname 'Abba Fatan' – 'The Quick'. It was only after a year had passed that I met my friend and discovered he was alive!

Most of the time we chose to hide in the bush so that we could fight better. We often ambushed on both sides of the road from Chilga up to Matamma, making it very difficult for the Italians to travel on it. To attack the enemy other than by ambushing was very risky as the enemy moved with strong escorts.

After the British came to our aid, we exchanged information, meeting at Acheraberr (along the Chilga–Matamma road) with *Ato* (later *Dejazmach*) Gila Giyorgis as translator and a British Captain called Folly, as representative to the small unit. A further discussion was held through our representative Mohammed Afandi, and it was agreed that 170 Patriots under Bayyu's leadership and 30 British soldiers would bury explosives along the road. The British set the mines as they knew more about it than we did, but we did help them to bury them. Afterwards, when Italian Blackshirts came loaded in seven vehicles, we were able to destroy them. However, after the explosion their forces following behind launched a strong offensive and we were obliged to evacuate the area. You could see the smoke for many hours afterwards, and the British officer took lots of photographs.

During this period, a number of refugee Patriots came from the Sudan and helped as messengers. Among those who came to our area were *Ato* Hiywot Hedaru, *Balambaras* Ashaber Gebra Hiywot, *Ato* Wolda-Giyorgis Tedla, Major Asegahegn Ar'aya, *Woizero* Banchiygezu Kidane (who gave us medical assistance) and *Woizero* Wagaye. *Ras* Wubneh Tessemma, too, as the supreme commander of the whole area, exchanged letters and summoned assistance at various times. Once, a brave Patriot named *Dejazmach* Wagnew Andargey was seriously wounded at the battle of Janora. *Ato* Hiywot and *Woizero* Banchiygezu sent him to Khartoum, where he was treated, and survived to see the liberation, soon after which he unfortunately died.

Our region was the one closest to the Sudanese border, and messages to the different areas in Gondar, like Gayint and even Shewa, passed through it. So, from the very beginning, we had external contact with the Sudan via the border towns of Matamma, Armacheho, and later Belesa.

Following Italy's entry into World War II, Britain came through the Sudan to help our liberation. After the Emperor returned to the Sudan from England, every Patriot leader in the nearby regions was called to the border and given guns by the British. These included Demetfer rifles, Lebens, hand grenades and ammunition.

We were not able to see the Emperor, when he first went into exile via Djibouti, nor did we get the chance to see him on his return, as he travelled via Gojjam. We did eventually get to see him though, when he was back in Addis Ababa. Through our region came such men as Tsehafi Te'ezar Haile Woldarufa'el, Major Bentinck, Langrose, Laurie (a colonel) and, the one who had come across the Gojjam region to spy on the enemy positions, that is, the British officer Sandford. Others included General Mar'ed Mangesha and *Dejazmach* Kebede Tesemma.

In Gondar, we were not the only ones; there were also many other Patriots organised under hundreds of *Dejazmach*s. And it was because the Patriots were so strong that the Italians, despite their better equipped forces, were only able to control the urban centres.

The British helped us with their weapons, officers and soldiers. In addition, they fought heroically with us. At first there were Sudanese and Indian soldiers as well in their armies but later on the Indians were sent elsewhere, while we fought on until Gondar was liberated. And the British fought with Sudanese Askaris and Kenyan soldiers who liberated Addis Ababa, the 'Jambo' as we called them.[1]

The British General Cunningham, who led the liberating forces from Kenya, had entered Addis Ababa on 5 April 1941, but since we celebrate the day on which our Emperor entered Addis, we take 5 May 1941 as our victory day. What still makes the Patriots of Gondar different is the fact that they fought on until November 1941, against the Italian General Nasi. He had refused to surrender and fought with numerous soldiers and better arms. He built a six-metre-wide barrier around the town, ringed with land mines, and tanks guarded the five gates. With the help of the British, however, we were able to break into his main fortress at Kulkal Bar on 22 November, and on 29 November General Nasi had no option but to surrender.

To augment our forces in the fight at Gondar, an army unit was sent to us from Shewa, as well as others from Tigray, Wello and Gojjam. This unit, known as 'Qundal', was commanded by the renowned leader *Dejach* Habta-Selassie. *Ras Berru* Wolda-Gabr'el came to the area as the Emperor's representative. A certain General Fox also fought with us, further reinforcing our attack with his two brigades of British and Kenyan soldiers. In the end, the Emperor's heir, Crown Prince Asfa Wossen Haile Sellassie, came to Fasil's Castle and heralded His Majesty's message to the crowd after hoisting our flag.

Most of the Patriots of Gondar province fought for about six years. But when medals were awarded for Patriotic service, it was only for five years' service. This was because the fighting was generally calculated as having ceased with the re-entry of the Emperor into Addis Ababa.

I was awarded ten medals. These are: the Five Years' Patriotic Service Medal, the St George Medal (for Valour), the Officer Star (honorary), the Omedla Memorial with the Victory Monument, the Silver Star of Victory, the Cavalry Star (honorary), the Silver 15 years' Service Medal, the Gold Long-Service Medal, the Star of British Infantry (for the Gondar campaign), and the Tank Unit Medal.

When we first heard about the return of the Emperor, we felt the way a released prisoner does. We were more than happy when we regained our independence, for the Italians had been slaughtering our compatriots, burning houses to ashes, and – worse than being colonised – they used mustard gas to attack us. Let alone our Emperor, in those miserable days we would have been happy whoever had come to our rescue! War is agony; it is not as easy as what we are discussing now. Added to the suffering we were condemned to bear from the enemy shots, we suffered from starvation, the blazing sun and fatal diseases such as malaria.

Better not to tell about what we wore! Any garment we found, we wore. If we could get them, we wore uniforms captured from the Italians. Apart from these, we wore shorts with a strip of cloth bandaged round our legs to protect them from thorns. Around our heads we tied a strip of cloth covered in butter. Other than these, Patriots fought the resistance half-naked! Concerning this, the Italians scoffed at us saying 'They don't have shoes; they don't have caps. They are wild animals!'

The entire nation was, in general, against the Italian rule. A few people had been bribed, and others with great titles had been forcefully appointed, but hardly anyone accepted the Italians of their own free will. The people of Ethiopia love their country and are brave. There were even Eritreans who deserted Italy after she used mustard gas at the battle of Maychew, and fled back to Eritrea or south to Gondar. Among these (estimated at about 1,800 in number) were such notable Patriots as Aman Andom and Major Wolda Qal.

Even though I have now forgotten much of it, I remember that we used to chant the following war song:

> This is the one who is called Adme Zeleke,
> Ask him his story for it is fantastic;
> When told 'an army is marching', he feels like laughing,
> When hit in the forehead with the enemy's bullet –
> Let alone Italy, even Germany was amazed.
> Never neglects little men, nor is afraid of big ones,
> He doesn't conspire and dislikes backbiting;
> 'Drink this milk' his mother said,
> Honey as a child the killer was fed;
> The calf whose milk Adme Zeleke drinks,
> Takes another's rifle and with that, it kills.

After the final victory of Gondar, young Patriots, myself included, were admitted to a military school, as His Highness the Crown Prince had arranged it for us while he was there. However, as trainee cadets the students were undisciplined, which caused the school to be closed. So, I made my way back to Gondar, where His Highness was still present, and went to Wello and up to Addis Ababa with him. This was still in 1941. For the next two years I rendered military service, and from 1943 onwards I was permanently employed in the Palace as a receptionist and then as a member of the Emperor's accompanying unit. In 1949 His Highness encountered danger as a conflict broke out between the Oromo and Amhara of Efrata (north-eastern Shewa) while he was heading to Wello. I was sent to the area with others to resolve the conflict. From then on I served as an administrator in different posts in seven different *awraja*s.

I remember when I first met the Emperor, he had a very noble appearance, yet he talked to people in an amazingly simple manner.

Doing something for one's country's glory, and being patriotic, is never determined by age. What I would like to forward to this generation is this, as a certain man from my folk once chanted:

> Allow me to follow and let me follow you,
> For it is the branch-wood [kindling] that helps the log burn.

I was able to be part of history, volunteering from my childhood and leaving the church education I was receiving. The youth, therefore, have the ability to stand and toil for the country's glory. It is just as the Emperor once said, 'Saying "I was born into a prominent family" or "I am a child of a lord!" is immaterial. What is more important is making oneself into a great thing!' Yes, it is the trunk which is greater in every aspect than its branches, like Emperor Tewodros replied when an English journalist asked where his line of descent came from, 'It starts from me, Tewodros, the trunk.'

I am now aging, but I thank God because those days have passed and by providence I am still alive to see all this today;

for who could replace those great Patriots whose feet we kissed and who were feared like lions. My pride is the sacrifice I have made for my country, and making history by defending its independence which can be seen to this day.

NOTES

1. *Jambo*, the Swahili word of greeting, equivalent to 'Hello'. Ethiopians, hearing it uttered by British troops coming from Kenya, used it by extension to mean the British.

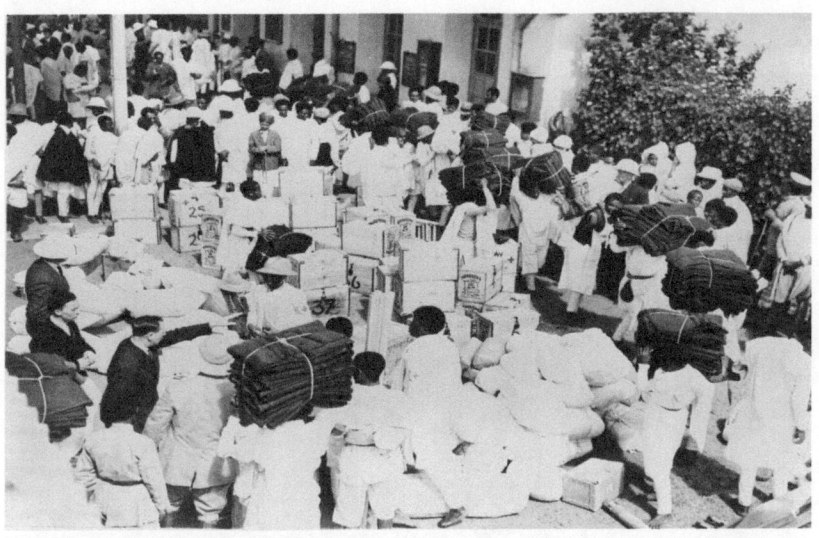

*Medical supplies for the front, including bales of cotton and blankets,
piled up at the Addis Ababa railway station, probably 1935.
(Library of Congress)*

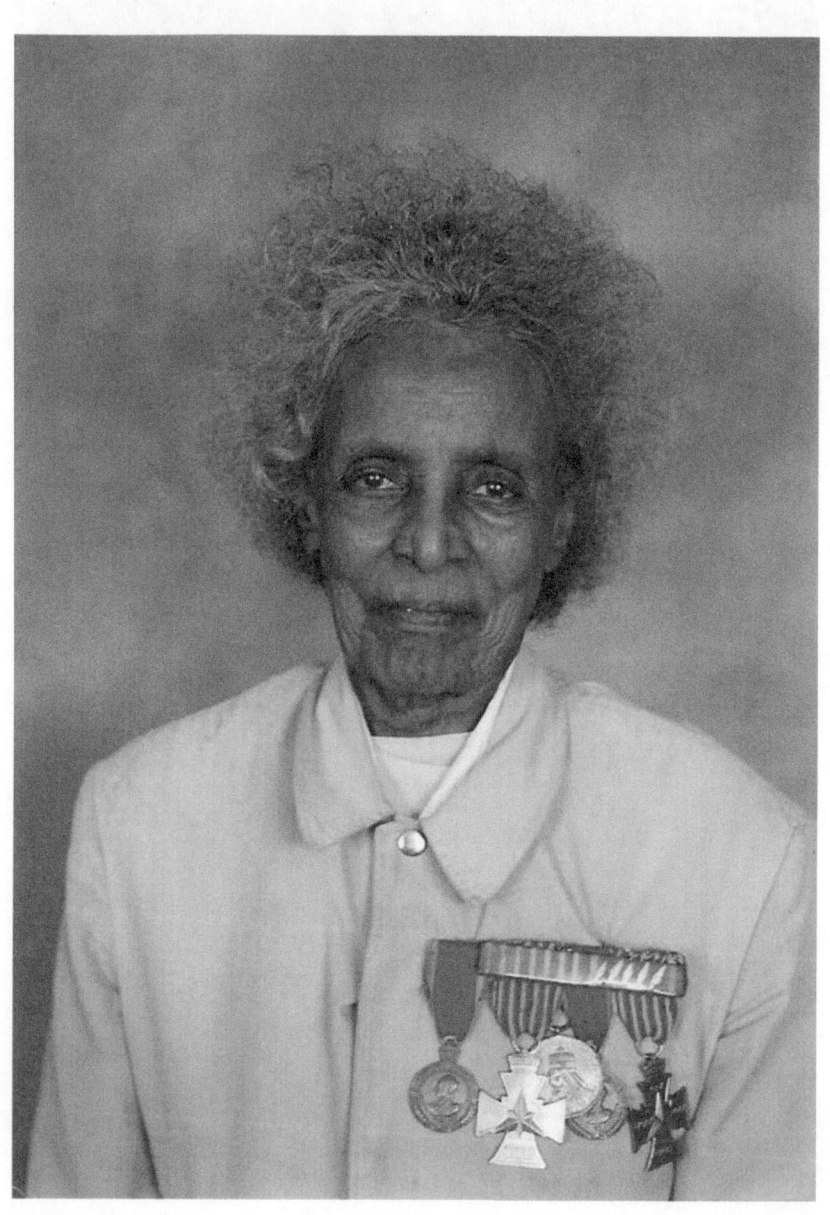

5

'THE EMPEROR ENCOURAGED US BY SENDING MESSAGES, SAYING "BE STRONG!"

Woizero Alemitu Mekonnen

My name is *Woizero* Alemitu Mekonnen. I am an eighty-year-old woman and an Amhara.

When Italy invaded our country my father, grandfather and brothers joined the struggle against the white men and killed the Italians, fighting not with modern weapons, but with such backward rifles as the Nas Maser, Senadir, and Wujigra. They did this until they were all killed while fighting, sixteen of them. After starting their struggle with those out-dated weapons they were able to get better ones like Minishirs and Albins from the bodies of the enemy, and by buying from the *Yewist Arbegnoch* as many as they could afford. My father *Fitawrari* Mekonnen Tebege, my grandfather *Fitawrari* Tebege and the others were all brave *Fitawrari*s. With my brothers Hailu, Melke and Tadele, and with their servants, they fought in great numbers.

One of my brothers, Hailu, was taken captive by the enemy as he ran out of bullets while fighting. Defying the common rule that prisoners of war should not be executed, the enemy killed him and threw away his body, which we found three days later with no teeth left.

We could not do anything but retreat to the deserts of Anto and Beresar Leqa, and stay there as rebels. From there we continued our struggle until the return of the Emperor from England.

All this shows that my family struggled beyond limit. I can even say they were among the pioneers of the struggle in the province of Gondar. They were from the beginning watchmen, that is, just like today's border guards. They used to keep the enemy in Gojjam from advancing across the boundary into Gondar, and vice versa. But despite this the enemy broke across the boundary and encircled them in Gondar. The encircling enemy force included Jicaria who led the enemy forces in Dabra Tabor, and controlled the Tis Abbay[1] and the bridge over the Abbay, and another enemy leader from Bahr Dar. My family members and relatives could now do nothing as they did not have any modern weapons such as machine-guns. They fought almost barehanded, but survived.

What inspired me to be a Patriot was the determination of our fathers not to see their country and the bond of their faith being invaded by a white power. And since Christianity at that time had strong ethical obligations I, and others, joined our fathers and started the struggle. I was approaching my fifteenth birthday then, but even a fifteen-year-old teenager could hit a target by shooting and throwing hand grenades, and performing other tasks.

The area I was involved in as a Patriot is called Wendogetmi, Sime Mariam. It was an important area in Begemder, close to the bridge and falls of the Abbay. It was also a place situated amidst the Italians to the left and to the right.

After my family were killed, the door became wide open to the enemy. In the fighting that resulted, traditional war leaders such as *Grazmach* Tedla and *Grazmach* Gebre were all killed. The army in which I was serving dispersed, but I survived and continued the struggle.

As I mentioned earlier, it was with Nas Maser and Wujigra rifles that we fought with in the beginning, but later on we began to use better and more modern weapons like the Albin, both the short- and long-sized, and the Minishir. We secured the latter guns mostly in the course of battle. Also, we once got some weapons, as well as bread and jam, by shooting an enemy aircraft down. This was near the town of Gondar where the Vincent,[2] full of weapons, ammunition, and provisions, was shot down while circling around looking for somewhere to land. It was tricked by our fellow Patriots who disguised themselves by wearing enemy uniforms and called for it to land. They then shot its tyres as it landed, and all the supplies it carried fell out as it crashed.

Our families used to teach us how to shoot and hit a target in our childhood. They instructed us to hit a target, usually a piece of paper or cloth, on a tree trunk. They taught every male and female child over ten. We would be scolded if we missed the target. They used to say, 'These lazy people are the ones who will give us to the enemy. If they do not fight with us, they shall die, and so shall we.'

Sometimes, when we were faced with an acute shortage of bullets we made a kind of bullet we called *kilis*. We made them by putting gun powder into the empty cartridge of a fired bullet and then fitting the bullet missile on to it.

Female Patriots like me bandaged wounds, and provided water and bullets by carrying them on our backs with a leather thong especially prepared for carrying, called an *ircot*. We would also inspire and encourage the males calling, 'Where are your retreating to? Where are you going? Are you going back to your mother's womb?' In addition, we would throw grenades from a distance by snatching its fuse with our teeth, as the men had taught us, so as not to get harmed. On top of all this, there was the notion that the country was going to be converted to Islam to lessen the grip of its faith, a notion that made our fathers rise. All the children and grown-ups followed their example and rose against the threat of alien rule.

Above: 1 *Italian planes in flight over Eritrea on 10 October 1935. They are of the type that participated in scouting and air raids over Adwa at the outset of hostilities and subsequently throughout the conflict. (Photograph courtesy of Corbis from the Bettmann Collection BE060355)*

Left: 2 *Camouflaged anti-aircraft gunners of the southern army of Ras Nasibu at a post in Ogaden, October 1935. (Photograph courtesy of Corbis from the Bettmann Collection BE060362)*

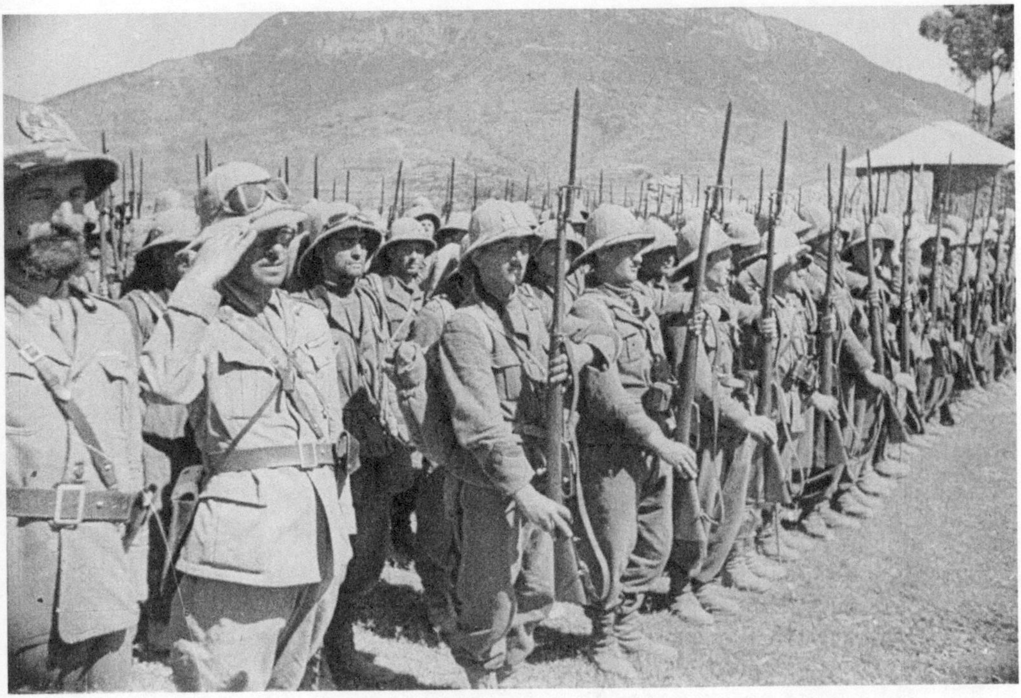

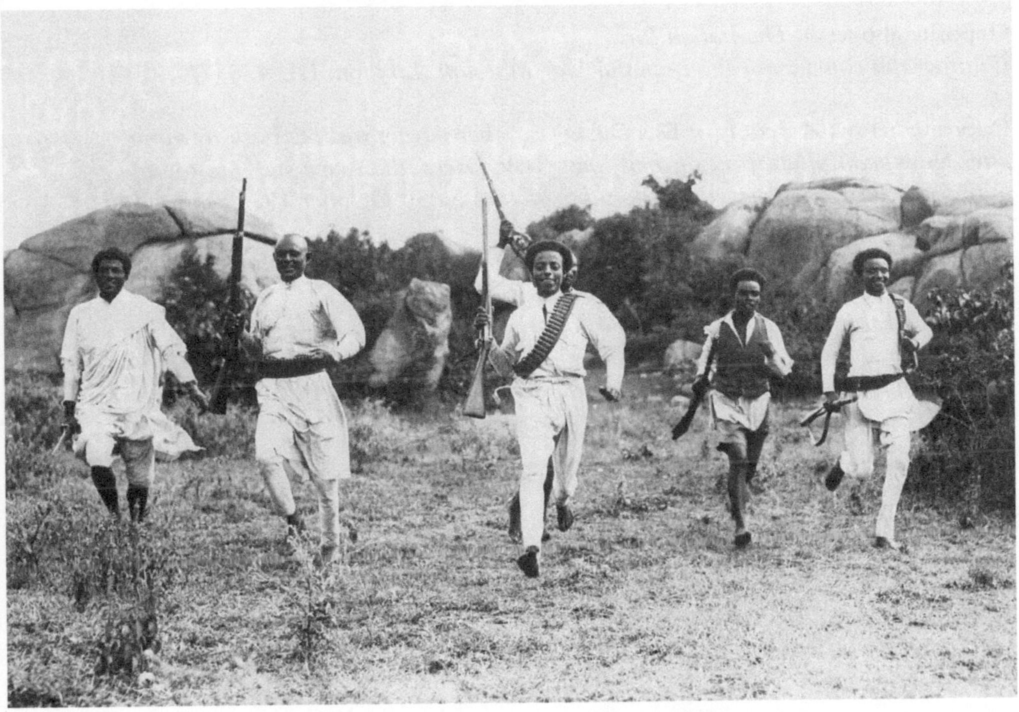

Opposite above: 3 *The Italian forces.*
(Photograph courtesy of the Imperial War Museum, London: HU 47657)

Opposite below: 4 *Scouts of Ras Dasta's southern army rushing back to camp after an expedition in front of their lines. H.V. Drees, the Acme staff photographer with the Ethiopian forces, who took this picture on 30 October 1935 reported that 'the Ethiopian never walks when he can run'.*
(Photograph courtesy of Corbis from the Bettmann Collection BE060371)

Above: 5 *Ethiopians of the captured Tigray province pay tribute, Italian fashion, to a banner showing a likeness of Mussolini, November 1935.*
(Photograph courtesy of Corbis, from the Bettmann Collection BE060344)

6 *Italian artillery firing on Ethiopian forces, the battle of Tembien, February 1936. (Photograph courtesy of Corbis from the Bettmann Collection BE053676)*

7–11 *The following extraordinary sequence of photographs shows an action between Ethiopian warriors and Italian troops, tanks, and the Spahys di Libya (colonial cavalry officered by Italians) in early 1936. (Photographs from the collection of Amedeo Guillet)*

7 *The Ethiopians, on foot and at a disadvantage in their white robes, confront their better-armed adversaries. Italian infantry on the mountain lay down a barrage as ten Italian Fiat Ansaldo light tanks (left) advance to outflank the Ethiopians. Realising their position is hopeless, some Ethiopian warriors (right) take flight.*

8 *The Spahys cavalry charges over the brow of the hill, and the light tanks push forward, completely surrounding the remaining Ethiopians.*

9 *Panicking warriors flee amid the Italian tanks, which are armed with twin machine guns, and the dead heap up (right).*

10 *The Spahys charge on, leaving the stranded Ethiopians to the Italian infantry.*

11 *Italian infantry pour down the hillside, while those Ethiopians who can still do so, make a bid to escape.*

12 *After the disastrous pitched battle of Maychew, a defeated Haile Sellassie abandons the front with his escort. He spent three days in prayer at the rock-hewn churches of Lalibela before eventually going into exile in Britain.*
(Photograph from the collection of Amedeo Guillet)

13 *Patriots and their transport.*
(Photograph courtesy of the Imperial War Museum, London: K1987)

Above and below: 14, 15 *Patriot forces wading across the Omo River
(Photograph courtesy of the Imperial War Museum, London: K1968 & K1982)*

Opposite: 16 *A small boy clings to his father's back during the river crossing.
(Photograph courtesy of the Imperial War Museum, London: K2005)*

Left: 17 *A leader of the Patriot forces addressing his men.*
(Photograph courtesy of the Imperial War Museum, London: K335)

Below: 18 *Patriot force during the advance from The Sudan, early 1941.*
(Photograph courtesy of the Imperial War Museum, London: K2829)

19 *The Ethiopian 'boasting' ceremony. The original caption for this picture states 'The walls of the crowd were broken by this old man with his spear and shield who cried great denunciations on the Italians and re-enacted the deeds that he and his fellow soldiers had done against the Italians'.*
(Photograph courtesy of the Imperial War Museum, London: K341)

20 *Patriots gather to watch the 'boasting' ceremony. Nearly everyone in the crowd, even the young boys, carries a rifle or machine-gun, often booty captured from Italian soldiers.*
(Photograph courtesy of the Imperial War Museum, London: K325)

Above: 21 *The triumphant Emperor is escorted into Addis Ababa on 5 May 1941.*
(Photograph courtesy of the Imperial War Museum, London: K1983)

Opposite: 22 *The Emperor, reinstated in his palace, addresses the Patriot forces,*
5 May 1941.
(Photograph courtesy of the Imperial War Museum, London: K2006)

23 *Central Addis Ababa today, showing in the background the Entoto Mountains where the Patriots gathered and the Emperor made his triumphal entrance into the city. (Photograph from the author's collection)*

Above: 24 *As the coffin passes through the Cathedral doors and into the crypt the Lion of Judah is finally laid to rest on 4 November 2000. (Photograph from the author's collection)*

Opposite: 25 *Old warriors stand guard as the Emperor's remains are transported to the Cathedral of the Holy Trinity for interment. (Photograph from the author's collection)*

26 *Detail from the 'Victory Monument' at Sedest Kilo, Addis Ababa, depicting the Lion of Judah holding the Ethiopian flag. This picture was taken on 'Victory Day,' 2007, which is celebrated each May 5th in memory of the Emperor's return to the city, and during which the veteran Patriots take pride of place.*
(Photograph from the author's collection)

As for me, I had enough reasons to keep on fighting the enemy. Our home had been set on fire and our cattle plundered. My family had been killed while struggling with the white enemy. My family had always been known for their bravery. One grandfather of mine was a follower of Emperor Menelik around Bahr Dar in Gojjam. He, *Dejazmach* Shefaya, was a brave man.

So far as our relations with Patriots of other areas were concerned, those from Gondar used to send cotton to those in Gojjam so that they could make clothes to wear. By so doing, we encouraged both male and female Patriots of Gojjam to work hard, side by side, and to fight against the enemy. In their close ties with the Patriots of Gojjam, the Patriots of Gondar met with the former and, whenever necessary, fought the enemy together.

The country folk took good care of us, for we were fighting against the Fascist force that had come to invade our country. In all the remote lands we went to, they would give us milk in response to our request for water. They did everything we asked and were, hence, *Yewist Arbegnoch*. As a matter of fact, you could say that all the people of Ethiopia were Patriots. Even the poor and the peasantry provided food to the Patriots and hosted them. They slaughtered sheep, and made meals for us which we would eat before returning to our struggle. What is unfortunate though, some deserters, and those who shifted to the enemy side for their own short-term gain, sometimes had the peasants who had helped us rounded-up by the enemy. To avoid this, we later began to send a single individual to bring us food when we were in our temporary bush camps.

At times, we were forced to face other problems in the wilderness. Once, in the narrow strip of desert called Anto, we were so thirsty that we were forced to drink filthy water from a pond through which cattle had passed. Moreover, we were often faced with a much-better-armed enemy with numerous machine-guns and cannons. But our Patriotic force was able to withstand all this, fight with the weapons it had looted from the enemy and even open an offensive.

We had no radios, so we communicated by letters stuck into a long stick split at one end. The letters reached the place we wanted in secret, without being touched by anyone.

We often carried out ambushes. We would make a small fortification from stones to hide ourselves. We would then extend only the muzzle of our guns through the wall and inflict a surprise attack. Unless they had been informed by bribed natives, the Italians would be taken completely by surprise. The Emperor also encouraged us by sending letters and messengers to us, saying 'Be strong!' He especially did this just before his return. In response we said, 'We shall be strong! But plead for help from abroad.' Indeed, he at last came with the British through Omedla and Sekela as we had been urging him.

It is possible to say that the entire Amhara people resisted pretty well. The area I was born and raised in, known as Aferwuha, as well as my own family have a particular history of the Patriotic struggle. Our fellow country-people are very fierce and they afflicted the enemy considerably. Once, I remember, a decree was announced by the Patriots saying 'Its [the enemy's] wealth to you; its hand to me!' Following this, we prevented the enemy from getting the fresh supplies of fowls, eggs, sheep and goats that it used to get so abundantly before. By aggravating the problem of supplies, the leader of the enemy forces in the town of Gondar, General Nasi, and his army were even forced to eat grass!

The engagement I shall never forget is the one in which my father lost his life. It was on the day when Saint George is remembered, that is 30 June. It is now sixty-two years since he died [1941]. What is amazing is that my father died after fighting so hard. The Emperor was by then commanding the war from the far south and my father died in a very desperate situation. I shall therefore never forget the grief I felt when I saw his death and those of my other relatives numbering as many as sixteen. For over a month I could hardly eat. Nor shall I ever be able to forget all the privations I suffered as a result of hunger and thirst, as well as from skin diseases.

When the Emperor returned, entering through Gojjam, I was in my home country, but my mother had gone with the Emperor and his allies, the British, to Addis Ababa. I came to Addis Ababa forty-six years ago [in 1957] and after having my contribution testified, received an award of two medals (the Five Years' Patriotic Service Medal and the Victory Star) as well as two thousand *Birr* and two *gashas*³ of land in Arsi province, from the Emperor. The other medals I wear today belong to my father. Thus, the Emperor has given me something I can still be proud of. He did not leave us Patriots aside and he has done many favours for us.

His Majesty had, above all, gone into exile so that the country would not be taken over by an alien power and colonised, because he was pushed by the Patriots. He was not fleeing, as some rumours have it. As for me, his going to England and returning with help was the ultimate in bravery and heroism.

The enemy, even while its final collapse was approaching, was disseminating rumours that reinforcements were coming to augment its forces. Moreover, they dumped large quantities of gold and silver into Lake Tana when defeat was close at hand. We also found human skulls buried in barrels in the deserted enemy fortresses in Kentero, Dabra Tabor, Tis Abbay and other places. We still do not know whether they slaughtered them, or even if they ate their flesh. People, including women, were killed outrageously by this cruel enemy.

I cannot sufficiently explain the roles of the female Patriots. There were some, including my mother, who commanded engagements as efficiently as their male counterparts. These women were none other than men. In Gondar, there were heroic women Patriots such as *Woizero* Simegn Kassa and *Woizero* Kibritu. My mother, *Woizero* Igigayehu, was so brave a woman that she was an inspiration to me. Her courageous father, my grandfather, who was an able servant of Emperor Menelik, influenced her greatly. He once led ninety-eight men in a fight with the *Derbushs*.[4] There, he ordered his men to take large slices of beef from the cattle he had slaughtered and commanded them to eat the raw meat in front of the invading *Derbush* soldiers – by so doing, he was able to make the terrified enemy retreat, shouting 'Here come cannibals!'

Patriots had to live on the gifts of the country people and sometimes suffered from chronic shortage of food. At one time, to express her exhausted patience with the privation, a female Patriot spoke to a male, chanting:

> Cut and eat your clump [long hair], *Fanno*.[5]
> As for me I shall get a man who has sown cabbages!

The chant illustrates the fact that the Patriotic rebellion and life in the bush had made the male Patriot, who would in peaceful times be the most productive member of family, unable to work; as the female says, 'I cannot eat your clump [hair]!'

I shall never give false testimony by saying that I have killed this number of Italians, or that this and that has happened to me. But I did in fact contribute a lot, from distributing provisions, making *kilis*, bandaging wounds, picking up those who were shot, encouraging those in action, and throwing grenades, as well as fighting occasionally with my Albin rifle.

What can I say? I have seen history. Somebody who has seen all the extreme aspects of life like I have should not live in the secular world. And today is not a day on which I should insist on living like this, combing my clump and strutting around. But for me, it is a matter of history. I am so proud when people watch us Patriots in our parades, and when they take pride in having us around. I really am proud of our history. The people of Ethiopia love, respect and cherish us. The new City Mayor of Addis Ababa has also recently helped and has given us better promises than ever before, thank God.

Obviously, we Patriots are now ageing. As we become less active, we pass on to the present generation the recommendation of keeping the country's freedom and frontiers we have preserved by recalling from history the hunger, thirst and offence we have tasted in order not to surrender and hand it over to alien rule. We Ethiopians will never give away what belongs to us, nor do we want what belongs to others. Our country is a country that has sent back foreign enemies by struggles of great bravery. This, in fact, is also attributed to our faith, otherwise we would not have had a force strong enough to chase an enemy away. The youth of today have to struggle as we have, and combat other plagues, such as poverty and diseases, by utilising the potential of their minds. And let God protect my country, Ethiopia, and make its borders fire, and its interior paradise.

NOTES

1. Literally, in Amharic, 'Smoky Abbay', the name given to the Blue Nile Falls, because of the spray rising from them.
2. *Woizero* Alemitu may be mistaken in identifying the enemy aircraft as a Vincent. The Vickers Vincent was a British RAF bomber used during the conflict (it was a sturdy but obsolescent single-engine biplane, with three open cockpits).
3. *Gasha*, a unit of land measurement: one *gasha* is equivalent to approximately forty hectares.
4. *Derbushs*, that is, Dervishes, or Sudanese militants.
5. *Fanno*, a term in general use at the time, meaning Patriot, soldier, or band of soldiers.

6

'MANY PEOPLE DIED WALKING INTO UNWINNABLE BATTLES'

Afa-Mamher Malak Negatu

I am *Afa-Mamher*[1] Malak Negatu. I was born in 1926 in the Lasta *awraja* near the place known as Maqet, in the former upper Gondar (now Wollo) province. I am now seventy-seven years old.

The Patriotic struggle in my area started as early as the campaigns in Tigray and the subsequent Italian victory [at the battles of Maychew and Lake Ashange]. While others soon recognised the Italian success and surrendered, the people of the area in which I lived refused to do so and became Patriots. Although I was somewhat young for this when it started (being only nine years old) I too joined the struggle and spent the next five years fighting.

I joined the Patriotic movement following the example of my mother, father and brothers who, with others, had started it in our area. During the entire five-year occupation, the Italians were completely unable to take control of the area, for it is a land which gave birth to numerous brave men and women, as well as *Dejazmach*s. During those years of struggle we offered indomitable resistance to the enemy. They in fact destroyed a good proportion of our gallant forces, but our response was far more fierce and devastating. This can be seen from the following song we chanted:

His country is Lasta, Shadaho, Maqet
Like the *teff* flour, he grinds the whites[2]

With the firm decision not to surrender our country to the alien Fascists, even children who were much younger than me fought alongside our elders. In so doing, we succeeded in preventing the enemy from occupying our area. A number of Eritreans (from Hamasen) also fought on our side and inflicted enormous losses on the Italians.[3]

The Patriot leaders in our area were men such as *Lij* (later *Dejach*) Yaragal, *Dejach* Gamoraw, *Dejach* Wande, *Dejach* Nagash and *Fitawrari* Abbay. Our immediate leader was *Dejach* Wande, and it was for this reason that we chanted the following war song, acknowledging him as our particular leader:

Servant of Male'ak [Wande's horse name], of *Dejach* Wande,
Tosses aside the whites like some garment,
With a local stick, Arabian sword, and black bullet.

We would organise our resistance depending on the strength of the enemy, as indicated to us in advance by the people of the countryside. When the enemy moved into our area in great numbers the countrymen and women would shout, 'Get the oxen down the hill that they may drink water!' This message had the covert meaning that the enemy force was unbeatable and that we should go down from the hills and retreat to the hot lowlands. On the other hand, when it appeared that we could easily force the enemy back, the people shouted, with its obvious covert meaning, 'Get the oxen up the hill that they may graze!'

At first we did not have enough weapons. A few of the Patriots had single-shot Wujigra rifles, while some of the nobility possessed the better Nas Maser. The enemy, by contrast, had the very modern weapons of the day like the Wechefo and Minishir rifles, as well as cannons and Belgig machine-guns. It was, however, only for a limited period of time that the enemy had the advantage over us of these strange weapons. During the later years of the struggle we were able to capture a great many such weapons, which we wrestled from the enemy with our obsolete weapons.

Sometimes we had to fight with our sticks and the very few Wujigra rifles we had. We did this by courageously encircling the enemy soldiers, provided they were far fewer in number than we were. Concerning this act of bravery we chanted:

His country is Maqet, in the lowlands,
He chases the whites with local sticks.

Where we usually ambushed the enemy was in the arid lowlands. We recognised the rocks of our district as Patriots, for they served as shields protecting us from enemy attacks. Besides, it was from behind these rocks that we carried out our raids against the enemy. The strong patriotic sentiment of the area further strengthened our struggle such that the entire area remained unoccupied.

The area was also a place known for its strict religious life. As a result, the people fought hard to keep their faith intact. The priests and monks often inspired and encouraged the people not to surrender their land or faith. This you can see from the following verse:

In Lasta, Lalibela's golden drums,
Cymbals and umbrellas paused,
When the weapons were enough,
Only in Nagala and the Maqet lowlands was the cross unspoiled.

This verse shows that, thanks to the resolute struggle of us Patriots, it was only our district that the enemy was unable to occupy and failed to disrupt the traditional religious system. Even the great churches of Lalibela were occupied by the enemy. We heard later that the Italian soldiers who had occupied the churches at Lalibela practiced rites contradictory to those of our ancient church.

One indication of the existence of a strong resistance movement in our area was the capture of Italian soldiers and, as *Kegnazmach* Agune Daraso often did, their transfer into the custody of *Ras* Berru [Walda-Gab'rel]. The rest of us also fought the enemy as best we could. Anyway, it was with the unfailing assistance of God that we were able to see the future. We obviously had hardly any strength to make a stand against the enemy – all the strength belongs to Christ.

It was just like some prey wrestling to escape from the grip of its predator that we struggled against the Italians. But, as was often the case, whenever we had a chance of getting the upper hand we violently destroyed them. The enemy's weakness was their failure to follow us to the end and destroy as many of us as they could have done. However, I cannot deny that they did kill a lot of our Patriots, while some of us survived only by chance to witness history.

When the struggle began most of us had only traditional arms such as sticks, spears and swords, and occasionally an obsolete Wujigra. Later on we started to get American-made guns, which we captured from the enemy soldiers. Gradually we began to fight more and more with the help of such guns. So, generally speaking, we fought the enemy with weapons which he had brought to fight us with. The Belgig rifle, machine-guns, cannons, etc. were, towards the end, fairly available to our country forces, having been taken as booty. To explain the fact that we fought the enemy to a large extent with his own weapons which we had captured, we sang:

As a wooden handle [of an axe] helps chop wood
So was the Minishir made by Italian hands.

While we Patriots conducted our struggle by ambushing the enemy, usually in the lowlands, the rest of the people in the district continued to carry out their normal day-to-day activities peacefully. In return, they cooperated with us in every possible way. They farmed while we stood alert to defend the locality from enemy attacks and attempts at occupation. Sometimes, however, where we were forced to retreat due to an imbalance of power, the enemy would invade our villages in large numbers and then leave after setting fire to the huts and other property. My own village though was never occupied nor suffered any atrocity.

It was not only on account of our warlike qualities that the enemy failed to occupy our area; it was also because of the inaccessibility of the arid lowlands and the absence of roads. Even today, the area is as isolated in many ways as it was in those days, so long ago.

What we usually wore during the years of our struggle were loose-fitting shorts, made of locally produced cotton. In the latter days of the conflict, some of us wore khaki uniforms that we took off the enemy – dead or alive. I can say that towards the end of the struggle we were ruthless in our treatment of enemy captives. In retaliation for their atrocities in the early years we took our revenge on the captured soldiers. We sometimes took away their boots and made them cross the arid lands barefoot. God forgive us our cruel acts.

So far as the battles were concerned, it was only until the first bullets were fired and the guns roared that we were scared. Once the firing started we cared about nothing and it was only if a bullet actually penetrated our body that we were conscious of the heat of battle. For this reason, innumerable Patriots lost their lives by throwing themselves into violent fighting.

During the five years' resistance struggle we had to fight many battles against the enemy. Thanks to the compassion of God the years of strife at last came to an end, even though many of our compatriots were martyred in the struggle. However, what is pitiful is that *Dejach* Wand-Wasan (*Ras* Kassa's son) was executed after surrendering to the enemy, having been promised a pardon, despite the advice of the Patriots who had urged him to keep on fighting and reject the enemy's offer.

Our district was, as I have mentioned, arid and somewhat isolated. Hence we had barely any contact with Patriots of other regions. Only *Abba* Gabra-Yasus, a well-known monk living a secluded life in the area, occasionally encouraged us with the optimistic words, 'Have no fear! Makonnen's son shall return.[4] He shall come and put Ethiopia in order.' All the Patriots fought on, awaiting the Emperor's return with profound hope.

Towards the end of the struggle our confrontation with the enemy forces in the area grew fiercer and fiercer. In 1940 we fought our first harsh battle at Gadabe. This was followed by an engagement we made against a stronger enemy at Debeko. After this we fought at Tameru, and in Lasta at Lalibela. At this battle the enemy forces launched their most violent offensive inflicting much greater destruction on our force than in previous ones. The Italians even bombed us from the air, and it was only in caves and under cover of rocks that we could find refuge.

The region as a whole was a country of many heroes, and as a result it survived virtually untouched during the years of occupation. Even today people sing of how brave the inhabitants of the area are:

Our land is Maqet, and our river – the Takazze,
Nothing can affect us if we refuse.

Close to the time of the Emperor's return, several of our leaders travelled a long distance and contacted Patriot leaders in other areas. With this we began to hear about the broader situation, most notably the Emperor's arrival at Belaya. This gave

us strength, after which on 5 and 6 April 1941 we fought a
fierce engagement against the enemy at Wayra-Bar Abbo. Then
we fought at Diqala Amba where my father and my brothers
captured some enemy soldiers, whilst I, as a matter of chance,
captured a Minishir rifle. This gun is still with me. At the time,
my comrades sang with admiration:

I don't know what a Minishir bullet looks like,
But I will tell you after asking Malak [me!].

For the sake of our country's freedom we had struggled forcefully and, with God's will, achieved complete victory. Above
all, we were happy that we had contributed something to the
independence of our country. All else was of secondary importance to us, though some of our elders, including members
of my own family, did not have their patriotic contributions
recognised by the government, while others, like me, did. His
Majesty, later on, issued a decree granting us a *gasha* of land
as a reward for our contribution as Patriots.

Shortly before the liberation we heard about one of
Ethiopia's brave Patriot leaders, Balay Zallaqa (his horse name
was Abba Koster's). We heard that he was a charismatic Patriot
leader who gave the whites a hard time and destroyed many of
them. After independence he was made a *Dejazmach* (he was
formerly a *Lej*). Later, however, since His Majesty was sometimes too hasty in making decisions, he had Balay, the national
hero, executed in public! On my part, I feel that His Majesty
committed a fatal mistake in so doing. Anyway, everyone gets
back the value of the evil acts of his hands.

In addition to Balay, we also heard about the exploits of *Ras*
Abebe [Aregay], *Dejach* Kaffalaw, and *Dejach* Zawde, all of
them leaders of the resistance in Shawa.

In our area, Maqet, many people died walking into un-
winnable battles like sheep rushing silently to be slaughtered.

The people in general love their country to an amazing extent and admired Tekel [the Emperor] even after the demise of his reign. Even during the Derg regime in 1986, thousands, including forty priests, were summarily massacred on account of their refusal to recognise the new government by claiming unfailing allegiance to the late Emperor.

We could see our freedom at last, after having for so long struggled for our flag with the same spirit as our fathers at Adwa, and other battles. For only this, independence was satisfactory for us, and most of us soon after returned to our farming activities. As for me, I received a church education and thereafter became a priest as well as a peasant. And even though most of the great heroes have now died, we survivors are still proud of our struggle and sacrifice for our country's independence.

NOTES

1. A title given for a learned priest in the Ethiopia Orthodox Church.
2. He is referring to the Italians.
3. The Italian army included many Eritreans, popularly referred to as Hamasens from the district of that name. However, a number defected and joined the patriots.
4. *Ras* Makonnen's son, Tafari, that is, Emperor Haile Sellassie.

7

'IN FIGHTS WHERE BULLETS SHOWERED DOWN LIKE RAIN DROPS'

Captain Ayana Berre

My name is Captain Ayana Berre, and what follows is a brief description of the memories I have as a Patriot fighting for the liberation of my country from the Fascist Italian occupation following the invasion it launched in 1935.

I was born and raised in the province of Wallaga, at a place called Gidukebe, in Dembidolo *awraja*. I am now, when describing these memories, an eighty-year-old man.

My soldierly life began as early as 1933, almost two years before the enemy aggression, when I joined the Imperial Bodyguard. I was largely influenced and motivated by my elder brother who was already a soldier. Two years had not elapsed since joining the army when the Italians invaded our country, and with this my Patriotic life began. I thus joined my fellow compatriots and became a Patriot, ready to offer whatever kind of resistance I could against the invading enemy forces.

The first two years of enemy occupation were too difficult for the forces in our area to bear and the well-coordinated enemy attacks forced us to flee the area. For this reason, under the leadership of our superiors, we took refuge in neighbouring Sudan and reached Khartoum in 1937. Regardless of the limited success of our previous struggle at home, we continued our struggle from the Sudan.

What we first did was to plan a strategy for our struggle. We set up a committee to organise our resistance and it was the establishment of this committee that played a pivotal role in offering a concerted struggle. Letters from the exiled Emperor, for example, reached the Patriots at home via this committee in Khartoum.

In 1940, after the outbreak of World War II and Italy's entry into it on the side of Germany, the British Government sent its first material assistance of two wireless transmitters to the committee. I was sent from Khartoum to Gondar with some other Patriot refugees to hand over these sets to the Patriots at home. They were given to Radda Tassama, a well-known Patriot in Chilga.

With the exception of a few of us who remained in Ethiopia, the rest returned to Khartoum. Emperor Haile Sellassie had by then come there and was preparing for a strong liberation campaign which would be conducted from the Sudan with military assistance from the British under the command of two of their officers, Wingate and Sandford. It was decided that Sandford should go to Gojjam to pave the way for launching a united attack. When the Emperor decided to send some men with this unit, I was told to go with them. The Emperor's determination was more than a strong weapon for me, and for my fellow refugees.

Under the Emperor's orders I thus joined Sandford's small unit. Of the British members of the mission I can remember Critchley, Bentinck, Gray, Nott, Drew and Johnson. A small Ethiopian force of around 150 men under *Dejach* Kabada Tassoma was also sent with the mission. Together we crossed the frontier into Gojjam, leaving His Majesty in Khartoum.

The name given to this force was Mission 101. Upon its arrival in Gojjam a warm and joyful reception was given to it from the Patriots there. The force was now in a good position to launch offensive attacks from its camp at Faguta.

Wingate and Haile Sellassie reached the Ethiopian border much later than we had under Sandford's command. On his arrival at the small town of Omedla, just across the Ethio–Sudanese border, His Majesty hoisted our flag. Wingate, after this, became the supreme commander of all the forces, which thereafter was known as 'Gideon Force'. The small force of Mission 101 became a reserve unit under Wingate's command for the next advance.

Wingate led the march of Gideon Force from Belaya with the Patriots advancing ahead. The campaign in Gojjam's rugged terrain started with an engagement at Addet Madhane-Alam. *Dejazmach* Mangasha Jambare, leader of the Gojjam Patriots in the area, helped in protecting the surrounding area from surprise enemy attack, as he had from the very start.

With one victory after another, Gideon Force continued its struggle, its strength being augmented by the Patriots in the locality. Burye was the small town we liberated next and entered it. The enemy forts at Wan Kidana-Mehrat, Mankusa, and Jiga were also subsequently cleared of the Italians. Our force then reached Chereqa.

It was there that the enemy offered a strong resistance to our forces, making it the most terrible of all the engagements we had had so far. Notwithstanding the many casualties we had to suffer, the victory of the battle was finally ours. In all the actions we had fought until then, I had been close to Wingate, and this was sufficient enough for me to learn how extraordinarily brave he was.

Undeterred by the enemy's counter-offensive, our rapid and triumphal advance continued. So, within a short period of time, we were able to liberate Danbacha, Gulit, Wanka-Giyorgis, Addis [not the capital] and other towns along the road to Debra Markos. In an elaborate plan to free the town of Debra Markos, Wingate ordered part of the force (including me) to advance south of the town without attacking it. This section, under Johnson's leadership, was assigned the task of checking the advance of any enemy reinforcements coming from Addis Ababa. It was while accomplishing this task and fortifying a place called Denbukbay that news reached us of the evacuation of the enemy from Debra Markos, and the entry of our forces there. After this our unit went to the town and joined the victorious forces there.

On 6 April, His Majesty the Emperor, who was following behind, entered the town and at 3 o'clock in the afternoon he raised our flag. Just that same day, we heard that the liberation force advancing from the south under the command of General Cunningham had entered Addis Ababa.

The time for the march from Debra Markos to the capital came later that month, on 29 April. That day we began our journey with the Emperor early in the morning. Crossing the Abbay River on a temporary bridge made by our soldiers, for the enemy had destroyed the main bridge across the river, we continued our march via Goha Tsiyon to the town of Fiche. On 1 May we arrived at Fiche where we spent the next three days as the Emperor went to pray at the nearby famous monastery of Debre Libanos. After this, we left Fiche for Addis Ababa which we reached on 5 May, which was also the anniversary of Badoglio's entry into the capital five years earlier.

At Entoto, the northern gateway to the city, we received a solemn reception as we entered, escorting the Emperor. I cannot tell in words how exciting the atmosphere was and how passionate the people were on the Emperor's arrival on 5 May. I myself wept, to tell the truth, tears of joy once more like I had when I first saw him in Khartoum after his return from exile in England. Yes, for us our Emperor, who had so far been deprived of his right and legitimacy to be leader of the people he used to rule, was all the armour we needed.

After the liberation of Addis Ababa, the campaign continued as the Italians still controlled many areas such as the town of Gondar, part of Jimma and Wallega. Under the Emperor's orders I was sent to Wallaga with other Patriots to free the area from enemy occupation. By 1942 Wallaga was completely liberated and our mission completed.

After 1942 I returned to the regular army and served my country as a soldier in Gojjam. In 1950 I went to the Ogaden following the Somali invasion and defended my country in every way I was expected to. Thereafter I continued to render my military service up until my retirement in 1965.

In all the years I served as a soldier, I contributed my level best to my motherland and remained loyal to the government. However, I was to achieve promotion of rank only to that of Captain – I had to remain with the rank of Lieutenant, which I was given by Colonel Sandford in 1940, for eighteen years before I was promoted to Captain in 1958. And with this my rank was to remain the same.

Returning to the history of the liberation campaign, I would like to explain the fact that the march toward Addis Ababa by the Patriot forces, with coordination from the British officers, was not altogether smooth and easy. There were cases in which we had to face attacks from Ethiopian contenders of such note as Mammo Haile Mikael. At Burye, where we had to fight with his cavalry, we easily smashed Mammo's force. But at Mankusa, the enemy put up one of the most fierce resistances encountered by Gideon Force. Under Wingate's command we had to meet a stronger enemy, numbering as many as two regiments. This force was advancing towards Debra Markos from Bahr Dar. It was led by the Italian Colonel Natale who was trying to reinforce the town's defence before our swiftly marching force reached it.

A strong enemy attack was launched against our force. It was a highly coordinated attack supported by tanks and 'planes. Despite this, our force eventually succeeded in routing the enemy, thanks to *Dejach* Zelake Dasta, who bravely opened the road. The role played by Zelake with his 200 men was an important contribution, without which, as Wingate later explained, we would most probably not have been able to gain victory.

For my part, I have had other outstanding adventures, such as the one at the battle of Mankusa. Here, while I was giving covering fire to our force with my machine-gun, a Sudanese soldier suddenly abandoned his key position and retreated in fear. Wingate immediately ordered me to fight in this fellow's place. I, therefore, moved and re-erected my own machine-gun, destroyed the enemy offensive and pushed the remaining force back. For this, I was greatly admired by Wingate, who even recommended an award of rank for me, though I was, for some reason, unable to obtain it. In the fight at Dinbukby, too, I wonderfully avenged the killing of my fellows by shooting their killer dead. I also took his weapon and handed it over to my commander.

During the war time, my admiration of the great heroes like Wingate, who shook my hand and was so friendly towards me, made me proud and fearless, even of death. The memories I have of Wingate's bravery are still vivid and astonishing even to me. Once, following a suggestion from one of his soldiers that defeating the two-regiment-strong enemy force would be impossible, his reply, which I never forgot, was: 'The force I lead is that of Gideon. And Gideon is a man cited in the Holy Bible as Victorious …' Wingate was, indeed, a real soldier, a soldier who fought side-by-side with us carrying his weapon. He never gave much thought to protect his own welfare even in fights where bullets showered down like rain drops. Once, to some soldier who had urged him to get down, he replied 'I do not fear death! Because even if I die my name shall not.'

It was owing to such great soldierly qualities he possessed that fellow Patriots and I gave Wingate the nickname 'Traffic police officer of the bullet.' His extraordinary abilities that made him appear odd are what made his secretary once say 'I would rather be under the protection of the Italian army than such a mad-man.'

I cannot sufficiently tell of how wonderful Wingate was. He was, for me, a true fighter – not a perfectionist, as Sandford in many ways appeared to be. Nor am I able to do justice to the bravery of other British soldiers whose nicknames can better describe how great they were in their military performances. For example, the nickname we gave to Johnson was 'Abba Mela', which means 'Father of Remedy'. We so named him because, with incredible wisdom, he once saved the enormous booty captured at Debra Markos from being plundered and wasted by our own soldiers. Rowe [Captain K.H.] was likewise nicknamed 'Abba Jigsa', that is, 'The one who ruins enemy forts'.

Frankly speaking, the British officers were so compassionate to us Patriots. Often, they suggested that we should fight from behind so as to avoid being sacrificed before we saw the complete liberation of our motherland! It was also only after their coming that we could get adequate supplies of weapons and ammunition. They were, to be sure, of paramount importance for our struggle. The only weapons we had before the British came were obsolete guns and a few others obtained as booty. However, I must say that both before and after the coming of the British, our force had no formal military clothing or uniforms. We fought wearing shorts, *gabi*[1] and other traditional clothes.

These memories of the resistance are not my only ones. Anyway, I have never felt sad in all my life, despite its great many ups and downs, thanks to the reassurance and strength I get from recalling the great years of my past. I am, indeed, always joyful and satisfied as I count the memories of my Patriotic years as the most treasured possessions I have ever had, thanks to the Creator, God.

NOTE

1. Locally produced thickish blanket, woven from cotton thread and worn as a toga.

8

'I REMEMBER THE BATTLE AT BELAYA METEKEL WAS THE TOUGHEST'

Sergeant Hunegnaw Hareru

I am Sergeant Hunegnaw Hareru, an old soldier ninety-one years of age. I was born in Gojjam at a place called Shebel-Berenta, in 1912. I served as an active member in the Patriotic resistance in my area, in Gojjam, all throughout the years of the enemy Italian aggression.

My Patriotic struggle was driven by my determination to fight and, if necessary, die for my country. I fought for my country's freedom in Gojjam under my chief commander, *Dejazmach* Belay Zeleke, and others such as *Fitawrari* Teshale Almeu, *Azazh* Ayele Alemu and *Fitawrari* Enyew Alemu.

The enemy had control of large areas in Gojjam. For most of the period [1939–41], along with other Patriots in the area, I carried out raids, forcing the enemy to evacuate places. We would spend the night encroaching into areas under enemy control. Then, by opening a surprise attack on their camp, we put pressure on them so that they would leave, usually after offering only a short-lived response of firing until it was daylight.

We had good relations with Patriots in other provinces as well. Through letters and messengers, we used to communicate and receive encouragement from them. We were provided with weapons and bullets by our men who were assigned to the task. Enemy booty was the main source of supply. That enabled us to obtain better firearms, including modern guns and even artillery. What we had before the Emperor's return were the Demetfer, old matchlock muskets, and the Moskob.

We did not believe it when we first heard that the Emperor had returned from exile. I was sent by Belay Zeleke to receive him, taking three men to accompany me. After a journey of eight days and nights, we reached the place called Belaya Metekel where, with most of the well-known leaders like *Dejazmach* Kebede Tessema and *Ras* Mesfin Sileshi, we met the Emperor. The joy I felt when I saw him at Belaya Metekel was limitless and profound. From that time on, I became a member of the forces on the march to Addis Ababa. Following his arrival with men such as Danhamershold and General Minalu, the advance started. I then led my men forward with the Emperor following behind.

At Shebel, Berenta, Enese na Enebse, Goncha, and Sarmider, all the way from Belaya Metekel to Debra Markos, our force was able to achieve victory and restore the freedom of the land. As soon as we entered the town of Debra Markos, the Emperor hoisted our flag. However, in response to the great aspirations everyone had for the liberation of Addis Ababa by pushing forward our advance, the Emperor answered: 'Debra Markos, is also ours. Are we going to enter Addis Ababa in two days? We shall break the Easter-fast here.' So we stayed at the town for several days and did not leave there on Easter-eve, the day we entered it, as we had hoped.

At Debra Markos, I was summoned by the Emperor, who awarded me 555 *Birr* in coins and 100 *Birr* for each of the three men under my command. After all this, I sent my companions back to my long-time commander, Belay Zeleke. I, on the other hand, continued the liberation march to Addis Ababa with *Dejazmach* Kebede and *Ras* Mesfin, who had declared that I should go with them saying: 'Hune (my shortened name) will never leave us.'

The march from Debra Markos started, and we soon reached Debre Libanos having travelled across the Abbay. At Debre Libanos, a well-known monastery near Fiche, we passed the following two nights and then started the march once again. Finally, we arrived triumphantly at Entoto, the mountain gate of Addis Ababa. What I will never forget is that the moment we reached there, the Emperor asked for a telescope, looked down on the city from the Entoto, and said, 'This ass [the enemy], even though he tried to destroy the country, has actually improved it. If we had given him two more years [of occupation] we would have seen a miracle!'

When we entered Addis Ababa, the people received us with great passion and shouts of joy. We then went directly to the Palace and entered with the Emperor. After that, I served as a regular soldier and was employed in the Imperial Bodyguard.

I also went to the province of Wellega to take part in the continuing campaign to rout the enemy. But this was rapidly achieved and, as the enemy withdrew entirely, I came back to Addis Ababa. Years later, I also went to Korea and the Congo, representing my country, involved in the campaigns there.

Getting back to the Patriotic struggle, after joining the Emperor at Belaya Metekel, when I had as many as 150 soldiers under my command, I remember the battle at Belaya Metekel was the toughest. At Mankusa, we gave the enemy no way to do anything; and at Chereka, a battle where a great many lives were lost (especially from the enemy forces), I was right at the front with my Demetfer. Not only there, but I was at Degien too, where the enemy once encircled us, and I helped to destroy them. There are a lot more battles I was in. I was not an easy person. But I cannot remember it all now, for a long time has passed since then.

The supreme leader, the Emperor, didn't let my contribution and efforts go in vain. He granted me three large plots of land, one in Wellega, another in Jimma, and the last at Karagore, on the outskirts of Addis Ababa.

The first plot I used for seventeen years and sold it for a good profit; the second one I benefited from for five years; but the last one I could not legally own due to some problems. Anyway, I am a man who has been in plenty of great adventures. Yes, who was awarded that much? Only I was awarded such plots of land, at my level.

For my many heroic acts while fighting for my country, I received eleven medals. Of these, six are for my Patriotic contribution during the five-year freedom struggle, while the rest are for my contributions in the Korean and Congo campaigns, from my country as well as the UN. I can, once again, say without boasting that I am a man of great history whose large collection of medals can clearly attest to my bravery and heroism. Indeed, no other person, so far as I know, has received such a large number of medals; but I, for sure, did.

During the struggle I used to sing moving war songs like this one:

In that sloping and slippery land,
Bullets in one hand and trigger in the other,
He has an oath with his rifle,
His hand not to be compassionate, and his piercing
Weapon not to get loose.

Servant of the Emperor, servant of Belay Kostir,
Servant of Kostir, of the destroyer.
Let alone when singing, still attractive when retreating,
When Belay Abba Kostir says 'Go and do it',
Is when Hune Abba Mersu (my war-name) kills
The blacks and whites passing before him.

Women and peasants were also heroes, who contributed their share to the Patriotic struggle by providing local drinks such as *tej* [mead] and *tella* [beer], and inviting us to feasts of splendid meals. The coming of the British with Haile Sellassie, via the Sudan, to assist us was also very important for our struggle. They gave us weapons and greatly encouraged us to be strong by fighting beside us.

9

'THEIR BODIES FELL THERE AND WERE SUPPER FOR THE OWLS'

Ato Ayalew Asres

I am *Ato* Ayalew Asres, an old man of eighty years of age. I was born and brought up in Bure-Damot, Gojjam, and I am from the Amhara ethnic group with some trace of Agew.[1]

Following the death of my father in Tigray earlier in the war against the Fascists, I joined the Patriotic resistance at the age of fourteen, uttering with determination 'This [enemy] which killed my father will not refrain from killing me too.' As my home country was a land of numerous Patriots I joined them and so spent the next five years fighting in the bushes and gorges.

My first commander was my cousin *Grazmach* Zeleke Ingeda, son of my mother's elder sister. He was my immediate commander. My next senior commander was *Dejazmach* Almaw Workneh, who was governor of the *woreda* [sub-district]. The supreme commander of the entire forces was *Bitwaded* Negash Bezabeh. However, the one who controlled all activities and led the politics was my senior commander *Dejazmach* Almaw, who was also the spokesman for *Bitwaded* Negash. I was able to stay close to him, study the tactics of commanding an army, and become well acquainted with his talents.

We often confronted the enemy by ambushing along the roads, attacking while their forces were on the move from one town to another, transporting their many cannons, machine-guns, bombs, and ammunition. We hindered their free movement by these raids and so forced them to travel by road at night. However, they would eventually reach whatever destinations they wished. From these places they would try to convince the local people to fight against us Patriots. In such cases we would encircle and attack them, so they soon returned to the town, killing and burning whatever they could. In engagements like this, we were usually able to capture their weapons as we knew all the routes in and out of the areas close to our home. So, the enemy was attacked and defeated with his own weapons!

At the very beginning we had outdated weapons such as Senadir, Wujigra, Moskob, Wetterli and, rarely, Wechefo rifles. These were what we launched our fight with. Besides these, Patriots fought with swords, spears, clubs and sticks. Those fighting with sticks would try to capture guns during the skirmishes, but this claimed the lives of many of them. Anyway, the captured weapons were a great help to the Patriots later.

The enemy, on the other hand, possessed Minishir and Albin rifles, large and small machine-guns, automatic rifles, cannons, bombs, and artillery capable of shooting a target at a distance of 20 to 30 kilometres. Whenever the battles were fierce, they would call in aeroplanes by radio and would bomb the whole area from the air.

When I first became a Patriot I acquired experience as a follower of my cousin and commander *Grazmach* Zeleke. However, whilst running into the middle of a fierce battle intending to capture weapons, like others before me, I was wounded in two places, in my right leg and in my forehead. When *Grazmach* Zeleke told my mother, she took me to *Dejazmach* Almaw and handed me over saying 'Let my son stay close to you and be protected, for he is going to die.' After that, I was protected during the large-scale fights and suffered no further harm. A Wujigra gun was also brought to me, which I later replaced with a Minishir, with which I fought with to the end of the war.

Fellow Patriots in our locality were organised under a local head chosen to lead us, and heads of *woreda*s were in charge of the Patriots under the many local heads. Occasionally, there were conflicts between the leaders of different *woreda*s as a result of competition for the greater bravery and for spoils. Nevertheless, when the enemy came, we all fought together in harmony.

One thing I remember: *Dejazmach* Almaw once devised a plan to waste the Italians' ammunition as we couldn't match them in open fighting. To this end, he prepared our men who stood ready on the right and left side. Then, those in front opened fire; and after them, those at the rear (opposite) opened fire; and finally those on the two opposite sides fired respectively. After having fired from all four directions, we stopped firing. Silence prevailed. After this, the Patriots on all sides blew trumpets. The enemy responded by firing an infinite number of bullets with a sound that would deafen your ears. The enemy was confused as to which way to go and so they remained where they were. We then went to the homes of the nearby peasants, were given our supper, and returned to encircle the enemy again the next morning.

Most often, it was while moving from place to place that the enemy were attacked – if they stationed themselves in one place and erected their machine-guns, we would not resist them. The Patriots used trumpets to surprise the enemy when they were en-route. Thus the trumpet was as useful as the bullet!

The peasants in the surrounding area ploughed and harvested when the enemy were not around. In addition, they fed and hosted the Patriots. When the enemy came they moved their cattle and the female members of their families to the remote bush and fought alongside the Patriots with sticks or any weapon they had brought from home. Even the women occasionally fought against the enemy, and some of them were great heroines. They often rolled big stones from the hills down on the enemy convoys. These would smash the enemy troops, their transport and their guns, cannons and munitions. The enemy had no cars, though they later brought tractors for clearing the roads.

Priests too encouraged the Patriots by shouting, 'Side with your faith! Side with your faith! For an infidel has come upon you'. A priest called Memher Wolde Gebriel who was *Niseha Abbat* [the father confessor] of *Bitwaded* Negash was the first priest to join the Patriotic struggle by slaughtering his farm-oxen to feed the Patriots.

The places which we chose for fighting depended upon the topography. If we were to fight around rivers and gorges, we chose the low-lying area and attacked the enemy upwards. When we reached mountainous areas, we fought using it as a shield. In forests too we fought using the jungle as cover. We always fought by encircling and isolating the enemy forces. Otherwise, the Italians were unbeatable in frontal fighting and their shots were as uninterrupted as the blowing wind.

We did not have communication radios, but whatever happened, even in far away lands, we heard about it right away. For example, we heard about the death of *Abuna* Petros[2] within three or four days. What man could reach our area in three days travelling across the river gorges of Abbay? I would rather believe the angels of God who travel with wings were serving us as a radio sent from God. Nor did we have telephones. It was only towards the end that the Italians brought telephone lines to the area. But there was the practice of exchanging messages by travelling on horseback for short distances. Nonetheless, something faster but unbeknown to us helped us to hear every piece of news.

Since our area was close to neighbouring Sudan, our leaders accompanied fleeing Patriots there and received returning

Patriots from whom we often received letters from the Emperor which he had sent via the Sudan. Delegates sent to encourage us also came to our area. As an example, I can cite *Dejazmach* Kebede Tesemma. Also, once, a foreigner[3] whose name I do not remember came, comforted us and told us what was going to happen. He took our pictures and went back, having collected our signatures confirming that 'we are fighting in the jungles and gorges'.

One of the battles I do not forget is that of Sekela, Gish Abbay [the site of the source of the Blue Nile]. In the month of July, a year after the Italians invaded, two Italians opened the fighting with many more Hamasens or *banda*s declaring, 'The people of Sekela have rebelled. They did not hand over their weapons.' During the battle, Patriots of the area encircled and routed the enemy. None of them escaped. Their bodies fell there and were supper for the owls. This was the first fighting to take place in the region. Previously, in May 1936 a great and brave Patriot named *Lij* Geremew Wendawuk had started the struggle by shooting an enemy soldier dead and capturing his Minishir rifle at a place known as Kwarit, while the enemy forces were moving from Bahr Dar to Debra Markos. However, it was really after the large-scale battle of Sekela in June 1937 that the people in the area began to say, 'We are not going to survive', and so joined the struggle.

At Engibara, the enemy had a large camp. Between Engibara and Burye is the fast-flowing river of Tlily whose source is the watershed from where the Abbay River flows. The Tlily is a large river covered on both banks with bush. It is the area where I was born. Whenever the Italians went from Engibara to Burye, and whenever they returned, they raided the area along the Tlily. This was why such brave Patriots as *Fitawrari* Meshesha Yimer, *Fitawrari* Gebreyesus Ag'azi and *Kegnazmach* Birhan Belay, who were also born in that place, organised the local Patriots and started the resistance struggle, collaborating with my commander *Grazmach* Zeleke. After that, there was always fighting in the area.

Being greatly angered at the death of so many of their soldiers in the battle at Sekela, the enemy gathered an army from different regions and came to Engibara via Bahr Dar. While they were preparing to move to Sekela to avenge their defeat, we Patriots received information sent by *Yewist Arbegnoch*. As soon as we received this, *Bitwaded* Negash mobilised the army and ambushed the enemy at Gomerta while they were moving from Engibara to Sekela. Hence, on 21 October, 1938 the enemy was defeated and repulsed, and was looted. They never reached Sekela.

In March, 1939, again, the Italians came to devastate Sekela. At the time a Patriot force that had come from Shewa through Wellega under the leadership of *Ras* Mesfin was in our region. This force possessed Belgig and Demetfer rifles, machine-guns and other modern weapons. Having welcomed them, *Bitwaded* Negash conducted a three-day fight at Fagitta with the combined forces. The enemy was defeated in this fierce battle and retreated to Dangila, losing most of their weapons.

In April, a pugnacious Italian named Galoni, together with a Captain Natalia, came from Bahr Dar leading a large army to Engibara through Dangila and then through our Tlily to Burye. This strong army was supported by aeroplanes from Gondar and Shewa which bombarded the right and left sides as it moved. At Burye, Natalia established his camp. Meanwhile, Galoni, moved up through Gewcha [later named Finote Selam] to Aswagudera, spent Easter there and entered Kesela, after dropping poison gas from the air. In taking his revenge for the earlier rout of the Italians, at the place where he now stood, he indiscriminately massacred many people, men, women and children. He then camped and remained there for some time, after which he left, assigning a force to stay behind to fortify the camp. While trying to move across a place called Enzora, this man (rumoured to have been one-eyed) was attacked by *Bitwaded* Mengesha Jembere, leader of the Patriots around Bahr Dar. In the engagement, some 70 or 80 artillery pieces, and numerous machine-guns and hand grenades, were captured from the enemy.

Afterwards a great many fights took place up until February 1941, when the enemy evacuated the area for good, and retreated to Debra Markos. They suffered repeated losses towards the end.

As for me, I do not feel comfortable in claiming that I acted heroically in any particular action. However, I can tell you about how I got wounded while trying to capture the enemy's weapons. First, I saw an Italian soldier fall, having been shot. So, I ran up the hill, which was called Mistcan, where he had fallen, intending to capture his gun. When I reached the hill, however, I missed the place. At this time, one of the enemy saw me from the hill across from the one where I was and fired a cannon at me. I sprang up and sheltered behind a tree, half of which was cut away by the cannon. I was wounded and knocked unconscious, and woke up long afterwards, at night. In the meantime, people who were close to me were mourning. My mother and my commander, *Grazmach* Zeleke, were stricken with grief, concluding that I was dead. But when I returned with my leg bleeding there was much happiness and shouts of joy. I was ill for many days, as there was no doctor around, and eventually I recovered with the help of whatever local medicine was available. As I was protected in all our following battles under *Dejazmach* Almaw, I did not have any significant adventures other than the one I have mentioned.

I knew men like my brother-in-law *Kegnazmach* Tefera Zegeye, who was an *agafari*[4] to the Imperial Government before the invasion and was appointed by the Italian administration to remain in that post. Even though I was only a teenager, I was sent to him to bring information about the Italians. This I carefully memorised and informed my commanders and it was of great importance in subsequently attacking the enemy. For this, I was taken by *Dejazmach* Almaw to *Bitwaded* Negash and awarded with honorific clothing.[5] I was praised and respected, for I had brought priceless information about when the enemy would come. This was valuable in enabling our forces to control key areas first and then to push the enemy back.

Near to the time of the Emperor's return, we received a message to collect weapons from the Sudanese border. Some men were chosen by *Bitwaded* Negash and *Bitwaded* Mengesha and sent to collect them and brought back Demetfers, Lebens, and other foreign rifles, loaded on mules.

In Gojjam, there were four supreme leaders who led the Patriotic struggle. *Bitwaded* Negash controlled the area extending from Debra Markos to the Sudanese border, mostly accompanying and receiving refugees with his subordinate *Dejazmach* Almow; *Bitwaded* Mengesha Jembere, the area around the town of Bahr Dar and the whole of Agew up to the provincial boundary of Gondar; *Ras* Hailu [Belskt], the entire Mota region and the surrounding area; and *Dejazmach* Belay Zeleke, the area from Debra Markos up to Abbay. It was because they administered that part of Gojjam near the Sudanese border that *Bitwaded* Negash and *Bitwaded* Mengesha received the weapons sent, with British assistance, by His Majesty, the Emperor.

Britain, under Prime Minster Winston Churchill, had offered us assistance with weapons (which were distributed among the better Patriots) and military officers, such as Wingate and Sandford. News of the approaching victory was spread by leaflets dropped by aeroplane. On 20 January 1941 the Emperor entered Ethiopian territory across the Sudanese border and hoisted our flag at Omedla in Gojjam. The Patriots were then on the one hand chasing the retreating enemy, and on the other receiving the returning Emperor, who was penetrating deeper into the country. At Burye, the Emperor stationed himself at a place called Achawsa–Wankidane-Mehiret monastery of

St Tekle Haimonet, which is surrounded by small rivers. Staying in this strategic place for some twenty-one days, he welcomed the Patriots and encouraged them for the next move. Since the enemy had not yet completely withdrawn from Gojjam, it was only when they evacuated Debra Markos that the Emperor was able to move there from Burye, via Dembecha.

It was while he was visiting a church that had been burned down by the enemy that I saw the Emperor for the first time. The day was, I think, a Wednesday and we were told about his arrival while we were in the countryside. Although he was naturally light-skinned he seemed very emaciated. His hair was unkempt and he wore a cloak. Because of all this, I had assumed that one of the better dressed people with him was the Emperor! Shortly after the enemy had evacuated our area, on 2 March 1941, the Emperor came and received visitors for many days. He also made speeches welcoming the Patriots. Hence, I was able to see him freely for many days. Melancholy and grief were clearly visible on his face, and he was reserved when he spoke. Occasionally, he posed questions to the lords close to him. As soon as I first saw him, I felt extremely happy, saying to myself: 'Oh! The Emperor is a man. He is a man!'

Even though I wanted to go with him from Burye up to Addis Ababa, my mother begged me, 'My son, why are you leaving me?' Others too recommended that I should not abandon her, and so I decided not to. However, I accompanied the Emperor as far as Debra Markos before I turned back. We had travelled from Wankidane Mehiret, via Burye, to Finote Selam, where we spent a night, and then on to Dembecha, spending another night there, before entering Debra Markos. At Debra Markos, the Emperor thanked those of us who were to return and saw us off.

A year later, in 1942, however, I travelled on foot all the way to Addis Ababa. There were several units of soldiers in the city, including the Ye Arada Zebegnos Police, the Army of Ethiopia (camping with the British in downtown Addis

Ababa), and the Imperial Bodyguard (who were much better dressed and equipped than the others). After I learned that they were the private bodyguard of the Emperor, I went to the Geneta Le'ul Palace, now Addis Ababa University, and asked to be employed. General Mengistu Neway[6] recruited me for training, after which I served the Emperor for five years from 1942 to 1947 as a bodyguard in the palace.

Now that I am old I am amazed whenever I recall that history. The fact that I was subject to all this misery in my childhood and was forced to discontinue my church education because of the sudden catastrophe – the showering bullets and bombs – has given me some dark memories of those times, struggling against the Italian assault. On the other hand, I was lucky enough to see the return of the Emperor, the liberation of our country, and everything else coming out of that disaster, with God's mercy, which replaces that age of misery, and I thank Him for my long life.

NOTES

1. The Agew, a Cushitic people, pockets of which are to be found in Gojjam.
2. *Abuna* Petros was an Ethiopian bishop who accompanied the patriots in an attempt to recapture Addis Ababa on 28 July 1936. He was captured by the Italians in the ensuing fighting, and executed. His life was subsequently commemorated in two Amharic plays, as well as by two statues in Addis Ababa.
3. Possibly a reference to the Australian ex-Senator Lieutenant Arnold Wienholt. Travelling into Italian-occupied territory early in 1940 he described his experiences in an article which appeared in the *New Times* and *Ethiopia News* on 13 April 1940, and was also issued as an illustrated pamphlet entitled 'Unconquered Ethiopia'.
4. *Agafari*, a government supervisor.
5. It was common practice to reward feats of bravery with new clothing.
6. General Mengistu Neway, at that time a distinguished cadet, and subsequently, from 1955, Commander-in-Chief of the Imperial Bodyguard Army.

10

'PAPA, ARE YOU GOING TO DIE?'

Ato Abate Alemu

My name is *Ato* Abate Alemu. I was born in Gojjam, in Burye Damot on 16 August 1922. Although I was only a kid (I must have been about thirteen then) I spent almost all of the years of the Patriotic struggle with my father. After the enemy killed him, some four months before the Emperor came to our region, I continued my struggle until our country achieved its freedom. For the whole period I was under my father's immediate superior *Dejazmach* Bekele Kassa and the higher commander *Bitwaded* Negash.

We had never liked white men. We were not favourably disposed towards them. The coming of the whites [the Italians] to invade our country aggravated this attitude. They sought to rule us by suppression, but as one's country is one's lifeblood, we refused to accept this and rose up against them. This was what inspired me and made me join the Patriotic resistance against the enemy. We fought at many places from Burye to Dega Damot, to Ankesha, Kuch Gebeya, and in all places north of Abbay [the Blue Nile]. There was no place in the province where we did not fight. The enemy used to burn our houses and we lived, as a result, under the shelter of trees for many days. From Agew Mider to Sekelo, and from Sekelo to Gish Abbay Mikael, we carried on our struggle responding to the national cry '*Assista!*, Brave Men'.

I did not have a profound knowledge of any weapons other than those owned by my father. However, I used to follow the older Patriots, carrying a big stick. In our movement we never retreated, but kept on going forward, picking up the wounded and fallen. However, when the enemy came, equipped to his neck with modern arms, we would often move away with our cattle so as to avoid a face-to-face engagement. We only did this by saying, 'No to my country', and 'better to confront the enemy in conditions that are favourable to us'. Even when we kids were ordered to withdraw with the cattle, I did not stay for long but returned to join my father. Our fighting mainly involved ambush attacks from the mountainous areas we used to occupy.

I was the only son of my father. His other children were all daughters. He was an aggressive man, such that I sometimes used to curse him. He often sent me to bring him bullets whenever he needed them (shaving my then considerable hair to make me appear young). I would go to people who had deserted their country [the 'native troops' fighting for the Italians] and obtain the bullets they had saved by saying that they had fired them, and then came back to my village. It was because my father was their favourite (as he sent them *teff* [bread], butter, eggs and other items) that the deserters gave him the bullets they had saved. They hid the bullets inside sacks of cereals and loaded them onto the donkey which I brought from home for that purpose. Thus, it was by pretending to be returning from the market that I smuggled the bullets to my father. At home, I always quarrelled with my father because he would distribute the bullets that I had brought him among his retainers, who never brought any. I would ask him, 'Why do you give away all the bullets I have brought to your fearful retainers?' But his response was usually a whipping. I could do nothing but cry and then, after a while, I would become quiet.

Men like *Dejazmach* Bekele, *Bitwaded* Negash, *Fitawrari* Bekele Ambaye, *Fitawrari* Bogale Yimer, *Fitawrari* Yimer

Mersha and *Kegnazmach* Yehualow all criticised my father, saying, 'How can he send his only begotten son to be killed? Is this man crazy?' He would respond to such criticism, 'One cannot be two. A bullet does not enter without its will – it gets who God has meant it to.'

There were no modern weapons or radio transmitters in the hands of the Patriots. The weapons our father had consisted of a muzzle-loading rifle, an old musket and a Russian rifle. They were obsolete and time-consuming to load as some of them needed a rod to take out the cartridge after firing a bullet. Other better weapons were obtained only from enemy booty, and I remember these included a match-lock rifle, and one with a bayonet.

In our region, the enemy's main camp was the village of a deserter in Burye. This was *Dejazmach* Mamo Haile Mikael, a grandson of *Ras* Hailu. His main reason for turning against his people and his country, and allying himself with the enemy, was to take revenge for his father whom, he argued, the people in the area had killed in a fight over territory. Mamo had therefore led the enemy and other native deserters, and had carried out exterminations in Burye, Guagusa, Wenberma and other areas, in the years between 1938 and '41.

I do not exactly remember the dates, but I do remember the battlefields and fights where we were given orders to pick up the wounded or dead Patriots. In all those years, as I've mentioned already, I never left my father throughout the struggle.

Once, when we were going down from Burye to the lowlands of Lyew Mikael to bury my father's younger brother who had been killed by the enemy, two priests, Enyew and Bezie, who were going with us, were sniped at by the enemy. My father was also wounded in three places, but unlike the priests he did not die. It was long after this, in November 1940, that my father lost his life in a fight at Burye. It was *Dejazmach* Bekele who picked up his body. I will never forget what he said when I asked him, 'Papa, are you going to die?'

'I shall not die,' he replied, 'I'm just resting until we pass this place.'

My father, *Kegnazmech* Alemu Endalamaw, was the eldest in his family of six sons. He was the only one left alive as all the others had been killed by the enemy before him.

At Burye, in the middle of the five years of Patriotism, I made a great commotion in the enemy camp and caused the Hamasen soldiers to fight one another by throwing a small bomb into the *demera*[1] of the Meskel feast on 25 September. I did this by entering the enemy camp disguised as a traveller. It was because of this incredible escapade that *Dejazmach* Bekele gave me my nickname 'Kebrit' which means 'The Match', for I had made such an explosion among the enemy, and then escaped safely.

When the Emperor was about to enter into Gojjam, messengers such as the old Patriot Ahana Birre were sent to us and explained that we should collect better weapons from a place called Belaya – the Demetfer rifles of the Jambo (as we commonly called the British) and the nice American rifles. Many heroes died of malaria contracted while we had gone to bring these weapons from Belaya. But, thanks to the traditional medicine made from garlic prepared by my mother for her Patriot brother and me, which I sewed into the back of my clothes, I was able to save myself and even others who were with me. This is what made people say, 'Alemu's son was saved, for his was only one.'

When the British arrived, the enemy had already begun to retreat. We were chasing them away, as we were the forward forces. This role played by our Patriots was pivotal for the British and the liberation campaign in general. Without such help from us, the British would have achieved nothing. The most important contribution from the British, which forced the enemy to retreat, was their fighting tactics. From Dangla to Burye, and then to Fanda Teekle Haimanot and further, they threatened the enemy, being on horseback, long before they captured each area.

Paradoxically, the enemy that had once been chasing us away as rebels was now in turn being chased. This situation continued until at Chereke there was a grave engagement between the retreating enemy and our force combined with the British, which caused a great loss of lives. Until recently, skulls and skeletons were still visible scattered around the fields there. In this battle, I stayed behind, but I fought actively in other battles like the one at Dangela where my father was shot by the enemy.

At the earlier battle of Tari Baguna, a splendid field in the Burye area, I was with my father carrying a warning horn and other equipment. At this battle, the forces of our region, we Mberma and Agew Mider, successfully drove Mamo's forces all the way back to their camp. I was a brave young man skilled in shooting. I never missed my targets and my bullets never fell to the ground.

At Shihun Kidane Mihret church and *Fitawrari* Bogale Yemer's compound, the enemy once sent in an attack and set fire to them. However, what I never forget is that *Fitawrari* Bogale caught the enemy on their return and chased them all the way to their camp at Mankusa. For their bravery the following war chant was sung:

When Boge's [Bogale's] rifle roared at Shihun,
Guay and Mankusa spent that night in panic.

Among the sad Patriotic memories that I do not forget is what took place when the enemy burned Whenterma by ambushing us very early in the morning. People had nowhere to escape to and jumped into the adjacent River Fetan. A great many died, both among the enemy and our own people. In this action a man called Mengesha Awgchew, having been shot twice, had fallen in the river, and cried out pityingly 'Finish me! Finish me!' However, the people looked at him in compassion and said, 'Why should we finish our fellow countryman?' Then they went off leaving him there. His reply was, 'Please! It will make you righteous, and avoid being condemned!'

To motivate others, I used to chant war poems that encouraged bravery and heroism such as:

> His father slaughtering an ox and his mother boiling water,
> His wife chopping meat, and saying 'please eat'.
> But his motive is as cold as a cork oak's shade.
> Entering like an owner,
> Into a house he did not build,
> The son of the unfortunate woman,
> Neither governs a country nor is he honoured.
>
> He's not a lion, it does not eat him,
> He's not an elephant, it does not break him with its trunk.
> So why does the man retreat, for a man's
> Will to fight them as God's is the victory.
> What is the use of going here and there,
> When bullets from there are sown here.
> When bullets from there are sown here.
>
> Just do your work being silent,
> And let observers tell and listeners utter.
> Do not provoke that well-raised man,
> Who pierces at one the tongue and chin.
> When the enemy came wearing clouds,
> He awaited it with loaded Belgig.
> And with the weapon, he hammered and wounded.

We had heard of the coming of the Emperor as early as when we were told to take the weapons from Belaya. But the story wasn't convincing to us and we didn't believe it was true.

Besides, although there were some eye-witnesses who said that they had seen him giving judgments, we hadn't received any letters confirming this as the messengers carrying letters in the customary cleft stick could not pass through the country easily and were often captured. It was at Finote Selam, after he had been received by *Bitwaded* Mengesha Jembere, and after he had come all the way through those other places, that we were at last able to see him for ourselves. Forces from the local Patriotic resistance around Ashewa, Gudera, Metche, Ingembra, Birray, Guta, and other places, joined him at Finote Selam, which in English means 'Place of peace'. It was indeed, for he came safely and he named it so saying 'The country is now peaceful up to here'.

The heroes of Wemberma, Agew Mider, Kolla Damot, Sekela, and Guder all came there as the Emperor stayed for some time. An aeroplane came then and dropped leaflets, which we scrambled for among ourselves. At that time, *Dejazmach* Almaw Workneh with *Dejazmach* Bekele Kassa (who treated me as a son after the death of my own father) chanted before the Emperor, along with his machine-gun, which he carried on a mule. The Emperor then asked what his name was and then said, 'Look at the mule! It acts like the man chanting!'

After all this, I accompanied the Emperor from Finote Selam up to Debra Markos. Then, while some kept on marching to Addis Ababa with him, I and the others turned back to our villages, for I was not as big as the others and we were told not to leave the home country a deserted land.

After this I started to live my private life. I am proud of what I have done for my country in my boyhood. And I also raised my sons in a way that they will follow my example. All my sons are imbued with a strong patriotic feeling. Had this not been the case I would not have considered them as my children. Yes! How is it that we can sit idle when an enemy invades our country? Where were we born? When the edge crumbles, the centre will became an edge. Saying 'No to my country!' is not the right thing. And a child who does not make his country respected is no child of mine.

NOTE

1. *Demera*, a pile of poles and branches used for a bonfire at the Meskel feast. Held in September each year, it commemorates the finding of the True Cross by the Byzantine Empress Helena.

The Emperor back in in his offices in Addis Ababa, 1942. Six years previously he had warned the League of Nations, 'It is us today. It will be you tomorrow.' (Library of Congress)

11

'WE HAD BEEN CUT OFF FOR SO LONG FROM THE OTHER REGIONS'

Grazmach Taddese Adamu

My name is *Grazmach* Taddese Adamu. I am eighty-two years old. Even though I was born in the town of Jimma, my ethnic background is Amhara, in particular of Gojjam.

When the Italian aggressors came, I was fifteen. When my father and others rose in Patriotism I, too, joined them with my Mauzer rifle and spent the five years that followed as a Patriot.

My participation started in the area of Kullo-Konta. The supreme leader of our army was *Fitawrari* Mengesha Hassen and his subordinate was *Grazmach* Wondimu Mulatie. During those five years, I served in such areas as Kullo, Konta, Jimma and other areas of Kefa province. Kullo-Konta is a region that is surrounded by bodies of water and, as a result, we did not give the enemy any space to enter the area until January 1936.

In January 1936 we fought with the enemy at Konta, under the leadership of the renowned Patriot *Kegnazmach* Haile Abba Mersa. In this battle we were able to defeat the enemy and push them back. A month later, in February 1936, they came to fight against us for the second time. In one of the engagements that followed, the famous leader *Fitawrari* Haile Abba Mersa lost his life; we were, however, still able to rout the enemy. For the third time, we had to fight with the enemy who now came in greater strength. On 3 April 1936 in Tocha *woreda* we had a fierce fight, but this time they defeated our forces, and captured the region.

Following this decisive Italian victory, we retreated and fled to the nearby jungle, where we continued our Patriotic resistance. Before this, we had made it altogether impossible for the enemy even to approach us, for we had until then offered a formidable defence.

In our Patriotic struggle we used a variety of guns, such as my Mauzer rifle, and others' Minishir, Nas Maser, Wujigra and the like. In general, all the weapons our Patriots fought with were obsolete. By contrast, the Italians used much better weapons like the Albin rifle, Albin-Wechefo, machine-guns and so on.

The peasants of the region were *Gebbars*.[1] During the enemy invasion they deserted us, as they resented the Amhara-dominated administration. In our area only we Amharas were Patriots. In fact, only very rarely did people of other ethnic groups fight on our side. Nearly all the Patriots in that region were Amharas, who lived by collecting tribute from the *gebbars*. My own forefathers had come to the area from Gojjam during the reign of Emperor Menelik. For this reason the local peasantry resented us, and sided with the enemy. Besides, many of the local community were pagans. They were not willing or ready to give any support to us Patriots. Whatever provisions we needed we therefore had to obtain from the bush. We hunted wild animals, and gathered root-crops like *ensat* [false banana] and *goddere* [sweet potato] from the forest.

Patriots of one locality had good relations with those of another. In Kullo *awraja* every Patriot developed good ties with others under the respective commanders of the Patriots in different localities. Accordingly, each and every Patriot in the *awraja*, being Amhara, knew and met with one another. However, we had no links with Patriots and their leaders in other provinces.

We never made contact with the Emperor by mail or messenger and we did not have any support from anyone. Sometimes, we heard a few items of news about the conditions in the northern and central parts of the country – in Gojjam, Gondar, Shewa and others. But this was very occasional.

Most of the time, we conducted our resistance struggle by ambushing the enemy wherever the landscape was suitable. This could be rocky outcrops, precipices, or whatever, depending on local conditions. Wherever we ambushed we sniped at the marching enemy forces and fought bravely against them. We would fire only a few bullets, but from every direction, thereby appearing to be larger in number than we actually were, and the terrified enemy would waste all their ammunition as they fired continuously in response. Afterwards, we would pick up the cartridge cases of the fired bullets so that we could reuse them.

What we wore were shorts, with a shirt and coat, all sewn by ourselves, as we had to make our own clothes. We wore no formal military uniforms other than these. We didn't have any modern military equipment such as communication radios and we weren't given any military information or provisions. Neither our own government nor the British ever gave us any such assistance. The resistance we offered in that area was entirely independent and self-conducted.

The enemy controlled all the towns and roads in the region, but not the deserts and jungles. The deserts were occupied only by us Patriots and the wild animals. From these strongholds we had secured we fought by ambushing. A great many women Patriots too fought with us against the Italians. Such brave women included my mother and her heroic friend who died with her at the battle of Gulo. Today, almost all of them are dead, both the men and the women.

Of the unforgettable battles I took part in, the one we fought in the month of February 1939 at a place within the

Zafa *woreda* stands uppermost. There we routed the enemy force stationed in the area. After destroying them with my friends I followed an escaping enemy soldier, shot him dead and returned with his Wujigra rifle. In Chenga *woreda* in the same Gofa *awraja*, we fought with the enemy and destroyed their camp, setting fire to it after killing an Italian-appointed native guard by the name of Belete.

The other battle I cannot forget is that of Gulo, fought on 6 March 1939. Encircling our forces during the night, the enemy raided us early the next morning. In that raid, my mother was killed. My two friends and I, however, spent the whole day fighting from a strong position. Eventually, the Italians withdrew from the area, and I buried my mother's body with the help of my friends at the spot where she fell. These are not my only memories, but the ones I remember most vividly.

Besides what I have told you already I remember we once carried out an ambush at Gercha, in Wushai *woreda*, Kullo-Konta *awraja*. We killed five Italian soldiers. On our side Tefera Ashagre was killed. But eventually we were able to drive the Italians from the area. We also confronted and defeated the enemy in Konta, at Zelba. All these battles have been witnessed and confirmed, so far as my involvement in them is concerned.

In my years of Patriotism I chanted various war songs, one of which was the following:

> The brave Patriot,
> Uncompromising to his enemies,
> And killing at once, like a painful disease.

Once, we fought the enemy by encircling their camp at a place called Kechkecha. While fighting, my friend *Grazmach* Zewdie and I saw an enemy soldier running away. We immediately followed him and after capturing him took away his rifle.

Again, in Cheta *woreda* I picked up a wounded fellow Patriot called Wolda Gyorgis from where he had fallen while we were besieging another camp, and took him to a safer place. As a result of my efforts he survived.

Because we had no significant contact with the Patriots in the other regions, and because we hardly heard anything going on anywhere else, we did not hear about the Emperor's return. It was only after he had entered Addis Ababa that we learnt the news of his return.

Even by the autumn of 1941, the enemy had not withdrawn from our area. However, having been strengthened by the news of the Emperor's return, we left the bush and succeeded in driving the enemy from the region.

That we had not heard of the advent of our Emperor was not so surprising. It was because we had been cut off for so long from the other regions, owing to the absence of cars and any modern form of communications. The pieces of information we occasionally received were brought by word of mouth, and hence took much time. It was in fact from an Italian-appointed native administrator that we first heard the exciting news about the Emperor. This person, named Belay, knew of the Emperor's return from the very beginning. Towards the end he cooperated with us, and we killed the Italians we found in their camps. We then marched from Kullo to Jimma to recapture it.

Following this, our commander, *Fitawrari* Mengesha Hassen, came to Addis Ababa and made contact with the restored Emperor. For his outstanding performance in coordinating Patriot activity and defending that part of the country from the enemy, the Emperor awarded him high appointments, after which he returned as representative of the locality.

Returning to my own history, I was employed as a soldier under the local government as early as 1932 at the age of thirteen. I did this so as to retain my grandfather's right to collect tribute from the land on which we had settled. I succeeded him, because he was very old. I was then able to maintain the ten *gasha* of land which served as our livelihood. I also inherited his rifle. I did not receive any formal military training before becoming a soldier. Nevertheless, we Amharas of the area were raised learning how to aim and fire guns.

Regarding the battles we fought, they were generally pretty fierce. They covered a wide area of the country and we fought at various places. We were often encircled and attacked, suffering heavy casualties. But we also laid siege to the enemy, especially in their camps, and killed many of them. Anyway, God's providence has let us survive and see today, without which we would all have been dead. Thank God! I have not been wounded anywhere, though I passed through a time of great misery.

As a result of the great resentment I had towards the enemy I often wished I could have annihilated them on my own, provided that I had the means to do so. But still, I fought with all my ability and do not regret anything. Besides, the enemy was not fighting alone against us. Many of the local people, the Balabats,[2] and their hereditary chiefs, collaborated with the enemy. They gave them information about us and pointed out our positions. Also, though only occasionally, they fought against us, using arms provided by the Italians. The reason for all this was their grievance against the *gebbar* system. Since they had been *gebbar* for many years they used the opportunity to attack us in a sense of revenge. Obviously, we Amharas were *Naftegna* from the start. This was the reason why we were resented, deserted and condemned to struggle alone.

However, after achieving the independence of our country, the Emperor rewarded us according to our contributions. By virtue of this, I was granted the right to own a *gasha* of land on which I subsequently lived by farming. But that was later confiscated by Mengistu Haile Mariam's regime.

It was in 1951, ten years after the liberation, that I was able to see the Emperor for the first time. After that, I served as a Member of Parliament, being a representative of the town of Jimma. But I wasn't satisfied in seeing the Emperor just the once, and for this reason I was allowed to stand at the Imperial Court, where I could see the Emperor every day from 12:00 pm to 1:00 pm, Monday to Friday. In this way I saw him for five years, from 1969 until the end, in late 1973 [that is, the eve of the Ethiopian Revolution].

Ethiopia defended her territorial integrity by pushing her enemy back through the armed struggle, thereby performing a history which nobody else in Africa has made. Her history is admired by all nations of the world. In the future, too, generations should know of such a glorious history and keep up the making of it by defending the country as we Patriots have done. This is what I want to forward as a piece of advice. Today, I have profound pride when I think of that great history. And indeed, the isolated struggle we conducted in our region, with no assistance from the British or our own government, is worth being proud of. Thank God I have been lucky to see today, unlike many others who have not.

NOTES

1. *Gebbars*, tenant farmers, in most cases traditional occupants of the land, who provided tribute and labour to the descendents of Menilek's occupation forces (the *Naftegna*) who settled in the region.
2. *Balabats*, local chiefs appointed to administrative office by the government.

12

'THE ITALIANS ARE SURRENDERING TO US WHEREVER THEY ARE'

Major Seyfu Haile

I am Major Seyfu Haile, a Patriot pensioner who has contributed his share in the Patriotic struggle during the five years of enemy occupation. I was born in Ensaro *wereda*, at a place called Dereko Mariam in the Province of Shewa in 1920. Before the Italian Invasion, as a young boy, I used to say the liturgy in the church, but when the enemy came in 1935 I left to join the Patriots.

I was, in fact, ignorant of what a state power meant at that time. I joined the Patriots because the enemy created terrible havoc by burning houses, looting cattle, and bombing the countryside, causing chaos in the villages and forcing us peasants to join the struggle. From that time until the end, on 5 May 1941, when I entered the capital escorting the Emperor, I was deeply involved in the struggle of Patriotic resistance.

Of the major actions that took place during the five years' resistance, the first was the great fight we had at Jihur in 1936. Our leader was the renowned Shewan *Ras* Abebe Aregay. We fought for seven days continuously. Later, the enemy encircled us, having been reinforced with forces brought from Jimma and other places. *Ras* Abebe could not remain there, and hence went to Ginde Beret. But I continued the fight with *Lij* Siyoum Gebre Hiwot and other Patriots by going back to the area around the place where I was born.

In my area there were a number of famous Patriots, including *Dejazmach* Teshome Shenkut, *Dejazmach* Gebre Selassie Adera, *Dejazmach* Yuilma Beshen, *Dejazmach* Shewareged Besheh, and *Fitawrari* Wondmneh, who is depicted in the statue at Sidest Kilo with the Italians holding his severed head. The statue was erected in memory of the victims of the Graziani massacre. I recognised him as I had been fighting with him and knew him, but many people do not know of this and are astonished when I show them this statue. Other well-known Patriots in other places included *Dejazmach* Kefelegn and *Dejazmach* Awraris of the Menz area.

On 11 July 1938 a fierce battle took place in which we successfully routed the enemy. Nevertheless, they soon returned as there was no other escape route on account of the river. Another engagement ensued in which I was shot in the thigh, the scars of which you can still see. My brother Feleke Wolde'ab was killed. Others such as Kebede Aydengtu, Wurge Nebro, and Gizaw Hiko also died then, after which we fell back. In the battle there was my commander *Lij* Siyoum, who led the fight himself, Yilma, Shewareged and many other daring Patriots. *Lij* Siyoum's wife Bishu, one of our women Patriots, was also with us.

We used to plead to God our Creator crying 'Give us back our country, Ethiopia!' and passed the days and nights so praying.

Mostly, we carried out ambushes. Two or three of us would snipe at enemy soldiers whenever we came across them, from ahead or at the sides, but usually from some distance away as we were so few. However, we also fought with them face-to-face when we had sufficient bullets and our force was strong enough. The bullets we fired never fell to the ground, as we fired with care, making sure we had clear targets, and thus achieved victory.

On the other hand, the enemy spent his bullets like water, with no attempt to conserve them. For my part, I say the

Italians did not know about tactics and were cowards. When we opened fire, they untied their mules and unloaded the bullets rather than firing in response. And it was in such circumstances that we managed to get bullets and weapons from the enemy as booty. What they should have done, had they known tactics, was to give responding fire rather than unloading their supplies and dealing with their mules, which in turn caused them damage. As it was, their reaction enabled us to raid them and capture their bullets and weapons, which gave us a source of supplies which we used wisely for a long time after.

The enemy had different rifles, such as the Albin and Minishir, medium as well as heavy machine-guns. By contrast, we had few weapons. Even our commander *Lij* Siyoum had only two or three rifles which he fired interchangeably. Later, however, when *Dejazmach* Tsehay Inku Selassie and General Tedla joined us, we got two machine-guns. But before this, our weapons were for individual defence only, like the Albin and Minishir rifle, short muskets, and others. My weapon itself was a long Minishir.

On 10 October 1939 another action occurred at a place called Bidigon, in Fiche *wereda*. An Italian garrison of battalion strength was stationed there. We were only ten men. We travelled in the desert at night and reached there at about midnight. We then daringly penetrated their defences, killed the guards, and finally came close to a certain *commandatore* [commanding officer] who was writing by mantle light. We wanted to take him captive, but we couldn't as he was very tall, so we killed him instead. Except for one of our friends who was wounded, we escaped unharmed. Meanwhile, the enemy was so confused that they were in a panic all night.

Having done this to the enemy, we returned to our own country. On our way we met Memher Gebre Selessie at the church of Alete Mariam. He was a collaborator monk who taught the people to say the Liturgy 'Weretu Hamanuel' which was related to the Liturgy in Mussolini's regime, instead of the usual one 'Meskele Egziabher' – Cross of God.[1] This monk had guards with rifles who opened fire on us on our way past the church. Later on, however, we took him captive and dealt with him down by the river. When we had finished with him he was not even able to walk. We could certainly have killed him, but we forgave him, and I heard that he became an employed priest after the Emperor's return.

18 October was the date on which a great extermination occurred and on which our leader *Lij* Siyoum Gebre Hiwot was killed. The enemy had a regiment stationed in the highlands at a place known as Wekolo and sent troops down to the lowlands where we were. We could not even look up, for the enemy held the high ground and fired down on us with machine-guns and artillery. We fought hard from 6:00 in the morning to 4:00 in the afternoon. Towards the end, *Lij* Siyoum fell, being shot in the forehead, and died. Many other Patriots were already dead by then. But we kept up our morale, and picked up Siyoum's body, and, after taking it by stretcher, buried it at a place called Seged Mikael.

On 16 May 1940 we were surrounded on four sides by deserters, at the desert area called Zegawedem. One deserter was at Mengesha Jebel in the direction of Fiche, another called *Grazmach* Belete attacked from the opposite direction, and others, like *Fitawrari* Wondimneh, joined in our encirclement. To tell the truth, *Dejazmach* Mershe was a bold and adventurous deserter who, by running ahead of their forces, caused havoc by throwing five hand grenades. We killed him, though, when he was reloading his pistol. A Patriot by the name of Aydagne who was armed with a Minishir rifle died that day. Another great war leader called Walelu Argaw, and Haile Cheber were also killed. I myself was shot in the foot, though eventually we all escaped the encirclement with a machine-gun we had captured.

An enemy soldier who was hiding in the church of Woyba Giorgis began to fire at our force, so we encircled him. *Lij* Siyoum Gebre Hiwot had not been killed at that time. What I remember vividly is the enemy crying, 'For [Saint] George's sake! For George's sake! For George's sake!' *Lij* Siyoum begged us to be compassionate, saying, 'Please! Leave him' for he loved St George so much and trusted in him. We knew *Lij* Siyoum loved St George, but we replied, 'Never! We will not leave him now that we have him surrounded.' But Siyoum had a well-known trumpet, and the moment he blew it we all pulled back. The amazing thing was that the Italian, who had begged for mercy, and to whom we had given it out of respect for our commander, then sent a message to the garrisons at Fiche and Addis. The next morning we suffered an air attack and enemy ground forces began approaching. Thus, the enemy we had forgiven for God's sake repaid us by causing us so much damage.

We all then retreated to the Zema river basin. Soon after, we burned the grass on both banks of the river and created smoke so that, by screening us and by running along the gorge, we could escape the air raids. Later, we were able to encircle the enemy, and attack him from the rear.

The enemy always attacked us by holding the higher ground. At a place called Gilgel Mikael, while my friend and I were a bit ahead of the rest of our force, the enemy opened fire on the fort from which I was shooting. I was wounded and, being shot in the lower jaw, lost three of my teeth. But the greatest pain was caused from splinters of cactus and spiny shrubs thrown up from the enemy's shots, which cut my eyes. My friends picked me up and then went back to the fight, leaving me at the Dalote Mikael church with a fellow Patriot. I remember a sergeant was killed as well that day.

My father came a day later and took me to a cave near the church. I could not eat any solid food for the following eight days. I was fed only melted butter from a gourd. Anyway, I recovered well from the wound, as you can see from my photograph, by using medicine from indigenous trees for the next two or three months. Leaders like *Dejazmach* Yilma sent me food during those days. As soon as I got over my wound, I returned to my company. However, I have not totally recovered from it – I still feel the occasional pain. Besides, I'm still missing three teeth in my lower jaw!

Among the adventures I have been in, the one I remember best is the one at Yetnora, where, after a battle, we were able to rout the enemy. There, the Libyan Arabs[2] in the enemy ranks were the ones who died in great numbers. I was searching for booty, and was separated from our force which was camped some distance away. While searching, I came across the bodies of two Libyan Arabs whose sex organs were mutilated. By their side, I found five hand grenades. With the two Minishir rifles I had taken as booty earlier, I returned to our force with a local country man who helped me to carry them.

When the Emperor returned to Goha Tsyon through Gojjam, we were at Nelemi, Fiche. With my friend *Ato* Lisanu, there were five or six of us. The Emperor sent a car to collect us, in which we were taken there. The Emperor was not in an automobile, but in a lorry, and his face was covered with dust. He was wearing eye-glasses, and armed with a revolver, and was escorted by Sudanese soldiers. We got closer to him with *Ato* Lisanu's guidance. The Emperor then asked us, 'How are you?' 'How were you hit?' he asked me, pointing at my chin. Lisanu explained what had happened to me. Then the Emperor said to me, 'Congratulations on your survival to see your country's freedom! How did you survive my son? How did you recover from your shot-away teeth?'

After this, we travelled to Fiche where we spent the night. The following morning, the Emperor went to Debre Libanos to visit the nearby church of Tekle Haymanot. And we, following his orders, began to march to Addis Ababa to wait for him there. We returned the car that had brought us from Nelemi, and took a lorry to carry the booty we had got at Deneba, and also the whites we had taken prisoner with their luggage. We finally reached the northern gate of the city, Entoto.

On the day of the parade, the Emperor came with two of his sons, Prince Mekonnen on the left and the Crown Prince on his right, with him in between. Patriots chanted war chants, and the people chanted too; some danced. The shouts of joy, the hand clapping, everything was so special. Seeing the joy of the people, we were overcome with excitement as well. At Shiro Meda, the people ran to him with great pleasure. Some people even died in the crush. The Emperor, now in an automobile, proceeded to the palace, with a warm smile as he travelled with his sons.

Majors, such as Desalegn, *Dejazmach* Yilma, and Tsehay Enku Selassie, were all chanting before the King when we presented the white captives we had taken. Among these Italians, one spoke French. The Emperor, therefore, asked him, 'How is it? How is the handling [of prisoners]? Have you suffered any unfair treatment?' To which he replied 'Nothing. No unfair treatment has found us, Your Majesty. We are much more respected than the people we governed.' This time, the Emperor mocked, 'It would have been better to have killed them.'

The following morning a British colonel with two captains and four Sudanese soldiers came and we handed over thirty-three Italian prisoners to them. Of these, one was called Gricco. He was, indeed, a pitiable soldier. With tears of grief, he showed us the letters he had received from his wife and father back in Italy. He said to us, 'Look! Mussolini did this to us.'

The coming of the British had not helped us to get weapons. Every weapon we possessed we had captured from the enemy long before they came. By then, we had great quantities of big machine-guns and other weapons. We were even giving away weapons to the countrymen who followed us. However, the British did help us with tactics. Once, two British officers joined us at Fiche, having travelled all through the hot-battle areas. They told us, 'The Italians are surrendering to us wherever they are. Let no-one from your side die from now on. Hold the areas where there are supplies of water and food. They will surrender when these are held.'

At Goha Tsyon, I felt a mixed feeling of joy and sorrow when I saw the Emperor for the first time. His dust-covered face, the lorry, his conditions were so pitiable. I still do not understand why he was in a lorry whereas other senior officers and officials came in automobiles. But the spectacles he was wearing, the Imperial Bodyguard uniform, hot with all the other military equipment he had, made me rejoice. He was young and handsome in those days. He was also very active.

The Emperor knew *Ato* Lisanu, my oldest friend, even before the battle of Maychew in the spring of 1936. However, at Goha Tsyon the Emperor found him tongue-tied. He asked him 'By the way, are you well? I heard that you were shot. I heard it on the way here from Omedla. I have kept a diary note of it, although I do not have it with me now.' It was after this compassionate dialogue and sympathy that the Emperor left for Debre Libanos giving each of us six *Birr* coins to buy supper at Fiche.

I never forget the war chants we used to sing; but some of the poems, I cannot easily remember. One that I chanted went:

Water is not scooped with a sieve,
Killer of Generals, yet in the future,
His father a lion, and the son a whelp,
Zeraf![3] Your servant …

After we escorted the Emperor to his palace, some of us served as guards there until the Bodyguard Army was reorganised. In 1948, I received my rank of Lieutenant from the hands of the Emperor in Hararghe after completing my training course. Sometime later, after another course, I became a Captain. And finally, with the diploma I received from Holeta Military Training Centre, I received my rank of Major in 1964, after the Ogaden campaign. What else? I have got medals for Five Years' Patriotism, the Star of Victory, the Menelik II, and the Empress Zewditu, for my contribution.

I am always delighted when I remember my history and country. However, I feel sad for the heroes who shed their blood, broke their bones, lost part of their body, and have done much more than me, who are now forgotten and are not given the necessary care. Personally, I thank my Creator that I survive to this age while almost all my friends have not.

NOTES

1. The suggestion is that the collaborationist monk sought to change the Ge'ez or Ethiopic Liturgy to honour Weretu Hamanuel, that is, the Righteous Emmanuel – an allusion to King Victor Emmanuel of Italy, instead of Meskele Egziabher, or Cross of God.
2. As well as Eritreans and locally recruited Ethiopian 'deserters', the Italians imported military units from Libya, its North African colony. Though numbers varied during the conflict, it has been estimated that the Italian force was some 340,000 strong, comprising a quarter of a million Italian-officered *Ascari*, or native troops, the remainder being Italian Grenadiers, Carabinieri, and Blackshirt militiamen. See Sierman & Smith, *Fire in the Night*, p.152. Perhaps the most colourful of the native contingents was the Spahys di Libya, a unit of irregular Arab (mostly Bedouin) cavalry, which took part in fierce fighting during the invasion, notably against the forces of *Ras* Imru at Selaclaca in December 1935.
3. *Zeraf*, an Amharic word expressing daring and resolute qualities.

13

'WE WELCOMED THE EMPEROR AT ENTOTO'

Captain Zikargae Woldemedhin

My name is Captain Zikargae Woldemedhin. I was born in Merabete, Shawa, in 1916. I am eighty-six years old. I served my country during the five years of Patriotism. The fact that some people deserted to the Italian side, and the others remained neutral when the enemy had invaded our country, made me determined to become a Patriot, and so I went to Moret and joined *Ras* Abebe's force.

As soon as I entered Moret, the enemy army from Fiche came, crossing the Ensero River to get control of Moret while the people were attending midday Mass. When the country men saw the enemy they confronted them and, by striking them hard, even managed to capture some rifles as booty. Shortly after the fighting began *Ras* Mesfin came carrying his machinegun. Once this was brought into action the battle grew fiercer. Then we had the enemy surrounded, some at gunpoint, some trapped by the impassable cliffs, and others who were lost. We had already captured eighteen men earlier, and now we added to these, and took two machine-guns as booty. The night fell shortly after this and with it the battle ended.

During this time, I had already gone to Moret, in Ensero, to participate in the Patriotic war from where I was living. Although I was not strong at that time I only had aspirations of heroism.

In February 1937 *Ras* Abebe stationed his force so as to cut off the Jirru area. There, the Italians were steadily encroaching with their large army in a single column, with the front section advancing while the one at the back took cover, and vice versa. *Ras* Abebe had fortified himself in a hidden ambush position and commanded his men, 'If any one tries to shoot, or say a word, I will kill him.' He had with him the soldiers of the Imperial Bodyguard with whom he had come to Jirru when the Emperor fled into exile. In addition, he had the local Patriot forces, including units that had arrived under the command of leaders like *Dejazmach* Awraris of Menz and some from Merabete.

When the time was right, he shouted 'Soldiers, open fire'. The enemy was destroyed at once and so successful was the victory that our compatriots were able to plunder all sorts of equipment, including capes, which we had never worn before, and even demijohns of wine!

The Italians organised another army and returned, but again our compatriots defeated them. I was not directly involved in the fighting as during this battle I was held back with the reserve units. But later, the Italians bombed our fortifications with an aeroplane, and many people died. In fact, later on, the Patriots succeeded in shooting down this aeroplane and it crashed into the Zeme, the river situated between Merabete and Jirru.

But *Ras* Abebe was not that successful after this and we later accompanied him to Gindeberet. In May or June 1938, men such as *Ras* Mesfin and *Dejazmach* Takele left because of the trouble the enemy was causing. They were saying, 'We cannot resist the Italians. We will have to go to the English [to the Sudan in the West].' But *Ras* Abebe said, 'I would rather die going East, not West' and so he went back to Ensero.

While we were on our way to Ensero, the enemy took *Ras* Abebe's wife and children captive, along with various supplies, while they were being taken on ahead. But *Ras* Abebe vanquished the army and went on to Kabi. There, the enemy ambushed him from a cliff top, but when he went into the middle of them with a grenade in his hands, they fled to Fiche from where they had come. In Jirru he hanged a certain deserter who was a ringleader, called *Fitawrari* Meshesha, from a tree. He then went across to Tegulet while we all remained in our home country. It was at this point that we joined *Lij* Siyoum, the leader of the army in our area.

I remember that sometime in 1938, at a place called Salaysh, we opened fire on a deserter by the name of Belete after encircling him. His wife was killed, but he fought back so fiercely that we could no longer resist and ran away. The fight continued and we fought at different fields, such as Gurtu and the Aletu river area.

A year later, in 1939, the number of Patriots had become overwhelming. We decided that (being over a thousand strong) we must not eat the bread of poor but must go and fight, die if needs be, and that those that survive would continue the Patriotic struggle. We engaged the enemy at the open field of Kabbi. They had stationed themselves there in great numbers. As a result, some thirty brave Patriots were killed, and several leaders, like *Dejazmach* Yilma, were wounded. But later, we bombarded the enemy and defeated them. Some of the Patriots began to castrate the dead enemy soldiers. This put pressure on us, and as we were also running out of bullets, we moved off and began to hide.

Later, in June, we entered Merabete, where we managed to push the enemy back even though he attacked us three times from his camp at Shetra. In September 1939, when we entered Ensero on our way back from Merabete, a large enemy force awaited us, surrounding Ensero by passing around Fiche. There, many people lost their lives. *Dejazmach* Yilma was wounded again and others, like Sisay Balcha, and *Le'ul* Seged

Azene, were killed. Our leader, *Lij* Siyoum Gebre Hiwot, also died at the cliff. We then fled through the lowlands, having escaped death, and entered Moret. There we elected our deputy commander, *Dejazmach* Yilma Beshah, as our main leader with the rank of *Lij*.

On our retreat to Silehi and Fiche, the enemy forced us from Fiche, Ensero, and from the lowlands, by chasing us away from the highlands with their army. We tried to get to Debre Libanos, but the enemy had also cut it off and this cost us the lives of six heroes, among them Demeke Fejyibeklu and Aydagn. But we threw twelve hand grenades at the ambushers and succeeded in capturing their machine-guns and other weapons which they left behind when running away. We then chased them, by coming from Kabbi to Debre Libanos, and so took control of the area. As we started our march upwards I took the rifle of one of our friends called Wondimu who had been killed. Later on, when coming down, I found an enemy machine-gunner who had fallen with his head in a well. I searched him and took a small pistol and thirty *Birr* in coins. I showed these to a friend who had joined me and we both shot at the Hamasen. The moment we hit him he cried out. I didn't know that he was alive, and I had searched him thinking he was dead!

We then went back to Kabbi, Ensero, and after travelling all night we were ravenous as we had not eaten for three days and our booty of the machine-gun and ammunition which we carried had made us tired. However, we were happy to have the machine-gun, which, after climbing a hilltop, we soon set up and fired to show the enemy that we had taken it. They must have been very angry!

Pay no attention to the minor battles; let me tell you about the major ones. On 1 September 1940, St George's Day, we arrived at a place where the enemy was waiting for us. They had captured some of our supplies as well as the women and the sick while they were moving ahead of us. As soon as we were able to manoeuvre behind them, we attacked and chased the enemy away and rescued our fellow men and women. Still, the Italians were observing us by stationing men to watch our activities. In such circumstances, my commander *Lij* Yilma, with whom I had carried a machine-gun, said, 'Go forward! Go forward! Go forward!' I replied, 'Where am I going, leaving you alone?' – I had no problem with going forward, but I was worried that he would be taken captive if I left him. However, his response was, 'Don't worry. Go!'

I promptly went forward and reached a place where some of the Italians were positioned, the main army having moved down to the lower land. I was a good shot, as I used to shoot birds, so I said to myself, 'I've got them'. Major Asaminew and *Lij* Rede had been ambushed and caught so I aimed over them at the white leader who, with a whip in his hand, was ordering the Italian soldiers to move up. I can still see it! I aimed at his knee and when I shot I actually hit his thigh. This is what always makes me happy. I then shouted to *Lij* Rede and Major Asaminew, 'Look at him convulsing! I shot him – You are my witness!'

In the meantime, three men came and, following them with the muzzle of my rifle as they approached us, I asked 'Who are you?' They were Hamasen who had come to avenge their wounded commander. They answered, 'What do you want?' and threw a grenade at us. It fell between my legs but it did not harm me. St George had kept me safe on his feast day. After this I shot once and we all fled, leaving the place to them.

However, the enemy forces in the lower area found *Lij* Yilma on his way back. 'Do not kill him! This is the leader' came the order. They then took him to Entoto with the wounded white man. *Lij* Yilma managed to escape and returned to our area. He told us that soon afterwards the wounded Italian died and in revenge the Italians killed six prisoners they were holding.

There were now rumours that the Emperor was coming and in response the enemy chased us from everywhere. We carried on struggling for some time and fought battles in various different areas.

Earlier, I had gone to my home village to visit my mother who was sick, after asking permission from *Lij* Siyoum, who had not died at that stage. However, after I had stayed for some days there, my own kinsmen said, 'If we do not capture this one and give him to the Italians, the other Patriots will come and consume us. We must have him killed.' When one of them ordered, 'Bring a fetter!' I uttered pityingly, 'If God of the Christians exists, let him bring judgment on you. I have not hurt any person here that you should think of handing me over to the Italians.' This shocked them, and while they were thinking this over, I escaped and took refuge in a gorge. Sixty-seven bullets were fired at me, but a friend of mine then opened fire on my persecutors and saved me. So, I was able, the next morning, to go across the lowlands of Merabete to Moret.

A year later, when I went back to that area with *Lij* Siyoum, I captured the man responsible for all this, being the leader, and seized a Demetfer rifle from him.

In the month of January 1941, twelve brave men, including me, were chosen to attack the enemy garrison at Fiche, and we were dispatched there. At around 10 o'clock that night we entered the town and killed every enemy servant we could get hold of. A white soldier then came out shouting, 'Take me prisoner! Take me prisoner!' A certain *Fitawrari*, Engeda Endaylelu, shot and wounded him, to which I added and killed him. After looting a rifle and a machine-gun we returned to Ensero via Debre Libanos.

On 13 April 1941, we fought until 11 o'clock, after which the white Italian captives we had previously taken at Lemi went and talked with the enemy fighters. They finally surrendered to us after the counselling they had had from their fellow men. We entered their camp and took thirty-three Italians prisoners, and booty of some forty machine-guns and many more weapons of other kinds. We then went to Fiche, with the captives being cared for, to welcome the Emperor. The town was, when we arrived, controlled by British soldiers who had entered Addis Ababa earlier. While we were there, we heard that the Emperor had entered Goha Tseyou. We then sent a messenger to him from whom we later learned that we had orders to await him at the gate of Entoto.

On 5 May, we welcomed the Emperor at Entoto in a solemn manner, in a line in which the white captives and the looted weapons stood in front of us. After this, we spent a night there while he went down to receive Patriots from other regions. The following morning, we entered Addis Ababa from Entoto.

After we had entered Addis Ababa, some fifty young men, of whom I was one, were chosen to be trained and we were sent to the palace. However, after staying there until 1942, we were sent to join the National Army. I served in the army for one year with the rank of sergeant and in 1943 I was transferred to the Security Forces. After five years with them, I joined the Police Force in which I attained the rank of Deputy Lieutenant in 1950, and Lieutenant in 1956. I finally received my Captaincy in 1961 from the hand of the Emperor himself.

14

'LARGE NUMBERS OF PEOPLE HAVE PASSED LIKE SHEDDING LEAVES ... BUT AFTER THOSE FIVE YEARS OF MISERY AND WAR, WE WERE ABLE TO HAVE A TIME OF PEACE'

Woizero Zenebech Woldeyes

I am *Woizero* Zenebech Woldeyes, an eighty-year-old woman. I belong to the Amhara ethnic group. I fought as a Patriot for five years following the Italian invasion. I was not yet fifteen at the time. My husband had fought in Maychew soon after the enemy invaded the country. After he came back I decided to join the struggle, insisting on never surrendering to the enemy, who was advancing swiftly. Within a short time the enemy had reached our area, destroyed our houses by fire, and looted our wealth. Not hesitating to fight them, I joined other rebels in the bush. I did all this in the area I was born and brought-up in, Bulga, at a small place known as Sichat Gyorgis.

In my life as a Patriot, I was at first under the command of *Kegnazmach* Likyeleh, but later on I continued my struggle under the leadership of *Ras* Abebe Aregay. I had had no formal training before I became a Patriot. With many others I rebelled and joined the struggle simply following the guns. We did not know fleeing. All we knew was going forward.

The struggle we had with the enemy was like squashing each other's throats. The enemy came forward, being well armed, and we awaited him taking position by lining up under a hill. We then attacked him energetically. Patriots from the area used weapons they had bought earlier and which they kept at home. The Government had only a limited number of weapons and these were distributed among those in the city. We were located far away and so did not get any. We only had Nas Maser, Wujigra, Leben, Demetfer and the like, though we also had some better weapons such as Minishir and Albin rifles, machine-guns and hand grenades looted from the enemy. Hence, we fought the enemy with his own weapons. My husband and I had a Mauzer rifle each.

We had close relations with Patriots from other areas. We fought by gathering and discussing together, and not by being dispersed here and there striving separately. Among the renowned Patriots around our area were *Fitawrari* Amare, Taddese Getabicha, *Dejazmach* Kebede Kassa, *Kegnazmach* Tafese Abanada, and *Kegnazmach* Tiruneh.

We did not conduct our fight by staying in fixed locations. We moved from area to area. I once went, for instance, as far as Ziqualla, some 50km east of Addis, near the town of Debre Zeit. Our force was in fact a detached prong, but by fighting with the enemy many times during the day we were at last able to hold the hilltop of Ziqualla, overlooking the enemy garrison at Debre Zeit. Leaders like *Ras* Abebe Aregay also led campaigns by moving from one place to another. Though I joined his force when he came to Bulga, he organised campaigns throughout Tegulet, Menz and Yifat.

There was no radio or other means of communication. We used to communicate by sending messengers. We got information about the position and strength of the enemy from our fellow country people. Accordingly, we could wait for them by following such a piece of information, and ambush them whilst securing the important entries and exits.

In the areas I fought in, air attacks were inflicted on the country forces in addition to the cannon and machine-gun fire. But we resisted all this with our own primitive weapons, and survived to the end without any assistance from the

Government or any other power. I participated in all the fights at Fikre Gimb, Wasil, Mesobit, Dofa Micheal, Aybamba and Nech Dengay. After we defeated their forces at the last decisive battle of Nech Dengay, we came out of the wilderness where we had rebelled, and started our way to the city.

Of all these battles, it was at Wasil that I carried out my most daring task. There, about thirty fellow Patriots died, hit during a bombing raid by an enemy war plane. In the midst of this, I saw a Patriot named Ishete fall, having been shot in the thigh. I then picked up this brave wounded soldier of the former Imperial Bodyguard Army, helped him lean on my shoulder, and took him to a nearby corner in the mountain lest he should be taken captive. When I did this, I still had my gun on my other shoulder. Not only this, I also encouraged the remaining force, shouting 'Be strong!' so that they would fight on, and not surrender.

How much can be told? If I narrate whatever happened each day, it would be too much. I remember once though, soon after I joined the Patriotic struggle, I was ahead of our force which was following along the way. All of a sudden I found myself detached from the rest of the army as I had gone too far ahead. I also discovered that I had got into the middle of the enemy forces. However, I quickly ran into the dense reeds along the bank of the nearby Kessem River, escaping the enemy who was about to capture me. For the following five days, I hid in the reeds, after which I made my escape and rejoined our forces.

In the areas where I fought, female Patriots performed many tasks in the Patriotic struggle. They picked up the wounded, prepared food, made coffee for their fellow Patriots after an engagement, bandaged wounds, fetched water, and encouraged the Patriots, saying 'Hit him [the enemy]! Hit him!' I cannot chant well, but we used to sing the following war chant to inspire our fellow Patriots:

The wild fig tree, the fool, bears fruit without flowering,
How can one of them fear unless the other is killed.
Let's hit! Let's hit him! Let's hit him, this is good!
Saying 'later' or 'tomorrow' rejuvenates the enemy.
Hit him! Hit him, and let him flee into the bush,
It's when saying 'I've got it' that a dog bites.

The country people, one can say, were themselves Patriots. They helped us a lot. They offered us food and drink, and told us, 'The enemy is coming this way' and encouraged us. The *Yewist Arbegnoch* also helped us, being in the towns and enemy camps, but we did not get provisions from them. What we ate were the bush buck, wild goat, antelope and deer that we hunted. These were sanctified by priest-Patriots before being slaughtered. As regards war equipment, we did not have many weapons, but the local people supplied us with bullets.

The important thing is that the enemy did not rule the country. They only stationed themselves in the camps and barracks they built by piling up stone fortresses on some of the hilltops. They never governed Ethiopia. The Patriots at large prevented them from ruling. Therefore, the enemy controlled only the towns, and couldn't do anything like penetrating deep into the countryside, or establishing new towns, or appointing local administrators. All they could do was to confine themselves to a few camps from which they used to shower us with machine-gun bullets every time we came up against them. Also, we used to snipe at them while they moved along the roads.

It was without any foreign assistance that we did all this. After a long time in this situation, we heard about the return of the Emperor and his entry through Omedla. Later we exchanged messages and were told to go ahead and await his return around Addis Ababa, so we started off for Entoto as we were told to do. Under the leadership of *Ras* Abebe, we got out of Bulga, where we were at the time, passed through

Chefedonsa into Sheno, and then to Debre Birhan, Deneba, Fiche, Sendafa and finally arrived at Entoto. While we were on the march, the Italian army commander in Gondar, Nasi, was putting up a strong fight. *Ras* Abebe then sent his subordinate commanders, including *Fitawrari* Tesema Wolde Gyorgis, *Dejazmach* Kumlachew, and *Fitawrari* Wodajo to Gondar, whilst he continued the march with us to Entoto.

Even though we had reached Entoto earlier than the Emperor, we didn't enter Addis Ababa, so as not to disturb it. We simply set up tents on the field there and stationed ourselves, looking forward to receiving the Emperor.

At Entoto, when the Emperor arrived on 5 May, I can tell you, the whole place saw happiness go beyond bounds. The field became full of flowers. There prevailed loud shouts of joy and delight. The profundity of that happiness cannot be told. What can I say? The whole of Ethiopia bubbled with joy. We, the Patriots, received the Emperor we were awaiting in a solemn parade. Our flag was hoisted, and joy overflowed. We then entered Addis Ababa and accompanied him to his palace.

When I first saw him, he was not wearing his royal clothes as he was coming back from the battlefield. I felt great joy when I looked at him. Not only I, but the whole of Ethiopia was happy. *Ras* Mesfin, *Ras* Andargachew Mesay and other aristocrats were with him. The British were also with him. They had got into the city as well as the Palace even earlier by motorcycle so as to discover the state of security in the city and to spy. I do not know. They must have been spying.

It was after a hard struggle that the other Patriots and I were able to see the Emperor. Many of the *Kegnazmach*s and famous Patriots I have mentioned earlier, including the heroic Haile Maryam Mamo, had lost their lives on such battlefields as Mesobit. But we survived the last battle at Nech Digay, during which we inflicted a great loss on the enemy, and were lucky to see all this life. At that battle we awaited the enemy in the chain of hilltops of Bulga, holding the main gateway into the vast plain of the interior. At first we took no action and let the enemy forces enter in a calm atmosphere. As soon as they reached the fields, however, we opened fire from the hilltops with seven machine-guns we had captured earlier, and sniped at them. The enemy, thereupon, fled and evacuated the area for good. Thus we were able to liberate other lands from the withdrawing enemy forces and make our way forward to Entoto where we received the Emperor.

At Bulga, the landscape itself fought the battle. The hills standing to the right and left like an army, and the low-lying plain with its water, were both favourable for war. Helped by this, we were able to get the upper hand over the enemy.

After the Emperor's return, I was awarded the medal of Five Years' Patriotic Service and of the Star of Victory for my contribution by him. And after those five years of misery and war, we were able to have a time of peace. Thank the Holy Saviour for living in peace up until now.

Ethiopia is a brave country and so are her strong children. Wherever they go, they come back winning victory. This is what I know. Patriots are not just those that one sees today. Many have died on battlefields. Heroic leaders have given their lives; soldiers of even far greater number have died too. Since the entire nation had joined the struggle, refusing to be ruled by the enemy, large numbers of people have passed like shedding leaves. Many of these, insisting patriotically on not retreating, were killed by the cannons of the enemy. It is God's providence that has made us people of today.

I will be antagonising others by this generalisation I know, but I still consider all white people as the same owing to the Italians' cruelty over us. They massacred us with their poison, scorched us with their bombs, set our homes on fire and plundered our wealth. I still remember all this. Also, though we were still in the bush, we heard about the massacre of civilians in Addis Ababa that the enemy carried out with shovels and hammers following the unsuccessful attempt on the life of the Italian [Viceroy Graziani] by Abraha Debotch [and Moges Asgedom] who threw the hand grenades at him on 19 February 1937. They were the enemy and so I still do not like them. I even get angry whenever the name of the enemy is brought up.

I recommend today's generation to follow our example and keep the respect of our country and its frontiers. In this regard, when the army of Sa'ebia [Eritrea] invaded our country [in May 1998] I was invited to encourage the young volunteers in my locality here in Addis Ababa. I consequently made a speech inspiring the volunteers and expressing my confidence that they would come back defeating the aggressor. As a symbol of my feelings, I presented our flag and a spear and leather shield to them, telling them that we too had gone to war when we were teenagers, and defeated an invader.

BIBLIOGRAPHY

Asher, Michael, *Thesiger*, Penguin (1994).

Bierman, John, & Smith, Colin, *Fire in the Night: Wingate of Burma, Ethiopia, & Zion*, Random House (1999).

Deedes, W. F., *At War with Waugh: The True Story of Scoop*, MacMillan (2003).

Del Boca, Angelo, *I gas di Mussolini. Il Fascismo e la Guerra d'Etiopia*, Rome (1996).

—— *The Ethiopian War 1935–1941*, Chicago and London (1960).

Mockler, Anthony, *Haile Selassie's War*, Oxford University Press (1984).

Pankhurst, Richard, 'The Ethiopian Patriots and the Collapse of Italian Rule in East Africa', *Ethiopia Observer* (1969) XII, 92–127.

—— 'The Ethiopian Patriots: The Lone Struggle 1936–1941', *Ethiopia Observer* (1970) XIII, 40–56.

—— 'Fascist Racial Policies in Ethiopia: 1922–1941', *Ethiopia Observer* (1969), 270–86.

—— 'Linguistic and Cultural Data on the Penetration of Fire-arms in Ethiopia', *Journal of Ethiopian Studies* (1971) IX, no. 1, 47–82.

—— 'The Secret History of the Italian Fascist Occupation of Ethiopia', *Africa Quarterly* (1977) XVI, 1–52.

Rubenson, Sven, 'The Lion of Judah: Christian Symbol and/or Imperial Title', *Journal of Ethiopian Studies* (1965) III, no. 2, 75–86.

Shirreff, David, *Bare Feet and Bandoliers*, London, Radcliff Press (1995).

Steer, George, L., *Caesar in Abyssinia*, Hodder & Stoughton (1936).

—— *Sealed and Delivered*, London (1942).

—— 'Official History of the Patriots', *Institute for Ethiopian Studies*.

Thesiger, Wilfred, *The Life of My Choice*, Fontana (1988).

Waugh, Evelyn, *Remote People*, Duckworth.

—— *Scoop*, Chapman & Hall Ltd.

—— *Waugh in Abyssinia*, Longman Green (1930).

INDEX